The Beginner's Guide to Doing Qualitative Research

How to Get Into the Field, Collect Data, and Write Up Your Project

The Beginner's Guide to Doing Qualitative Research

How to Get Into the Field, Collect Data, and Write Up Your Project

ERIN HORVAT

with MARY LOU HERON,
EMILY TANCREDI-BRICE AGBENYEGA,
and BRADLEY W. BERGEY

TEACHERS
COLLEGE
PRESS

Teachers College
Columbia University
New York and London

Published by Teachers College Press, 1234 Amsterdam Avenue, New York, NY 10027

Library of Congress Cataloging-in-Publication Data

The beginner's guide to doing qualitative research : how to get into the field, collect data, and write up your project / Erin Horvat, with Mary Lou Heron, Emily Tancredi-Brice Agbenyega, and Bradley W. Bergey.
    p. cm.
Includes bibliographical references and index.
ISBN 978-0-8077-5416-0 (pbk. : alk. paper)
    1. Social sciences—Methodology—Study and teaching. 2. Social sciences—Research—Study and teaching. I. Horvat, Erin McNamara, 1964– . II. Heron, Mary Lou.
III. Heron, Mary Lou. From the first site to the third place.
H62.B357 2013
001.4'2—dc23   2012042920

ISBN 978-0-8077-5416-0 (paper)

Printed on acid-free paper
Manufactured in the United States of America

20 19 18 17 16 15 14 13   8 7 6 5 4 3 2 1

Contents

Preface
Scouting the Terrain

Erin Horvat

When early explorers reached the shores of a new land they would send a scout ahead to explore the terrain. Scouts would do the hard work of mapping the terrain and come back and report on the country that lay ahead, identifying the best routes and warning of dangers. They learned where the rivers ran, what mountains would have to be crossed, and whether or not the "natives" were hostile or friendly. Explorers usually had no idea what challenges or surprises lay ahead for them in uncharted territory, so the scouts' "sneak peak" of what a journey through the terrain might be like was invaluable. I have often felt that students of qualitative methods needed a scout, someone who could let them know—in a detailed, accurate, and not overly romantic way—what it would be like to do qualitative research. I have also felt that it would be helpful to provide students with a better sense of what they might be able to accomplish in a defined period of time, as short as a semester or as long as the years of a dissertation. *The Beginner's Guide to Doing Qualitative Research* is an attempt to survey the journey for aspiring ethnographers and qualitative researchers—to provide a glimpse of what lies ahead.

Travel is often thought of as a mind-expanding experience that alters the way we see the world. Ethnographic journeys are no different. On ethnographic journeys we meet new people and understand the world in a new way: We develop a different perspective on what it means to "see" a social world. We develop an ethnographic lens, or as Carolyn Frank calls them, "ethnographic eyes," as we begin to see the world as a qualitative researcher.

As exciting as they are, journeys can also produce anxiety. When I travel, I often worry about whether or not I have packed what I will need. Will it be warm or cold—and will my jacket be heavy enough to keep me warm? Will I have to do a lot of walking—did I bring the right shoes? Will I fit in with the other people on the trip? Will I be able to find food I like to eat?

As a traveler I reduce my anxiety by learning about where I am going before the trip. I find out what the weather will be like and the basics of the local customs. And though it seems obvious, when I have what I need, I have a better trip. As an ethnographer you will bring along a suitcase of sorts as well. This book is here to help you decide what to put in that metaphorical suitcase—to reduce your anxiety and help you have a successful journey.

This book is for the novice, the uninitiated, the beginner. If you are thinking about beginning a qualitative or ethnographic research project, I hope that this book will be a useful field guide for you—a companion you can have with you on the journey that will help chart the terrain ahead. So get your walking shoes, raincoat, and rolling suitcase. Pack your good humor, patience, and sense of adventure. Join us as we explore the terrain.

HOW THIS BOOK WAS BORN

"Qualitative Data" was the first class that I developed when I came to Temple University as a newly minted assistant professor. At that time there was no course like it on the books in the College of Education. In fact, there was little support for qualitative work in my college. Like many academic institutions at that time (the late 1990s), Temple University was dominated by quantitative researchers. For the most part I think that many people at Temple at that time simply did not understand the kind of work that I did. I spent the first part of almost every research presentation doing what I think of as the "methodology defense" or "methods justification." How did simply talking to people qualify as research? Or, as one of my new Temple colleagues asked: How is this different from journalism?

Apparently these folks had not learned of the Chicago School of Urban Sociology's popularizing of ethnographic fieldwork in the social sciences and the long history of the qualitative tradition. As luck would have it, though, this lack of understanding provided several opportunities. Because there was no one teaching qualitative research, I could claim this area for myself. Thus, despite (or perhaps because of) the fact that I was relatively inexperienced at the time, I was able to develop the course and my ability to teach it. It also meant that I started teaching the course to small groups of graduate students (six to eight) and was able to work my way up to managing larger classes.

Looking back on these early days of teaching qualitative methodology, I am struck by my hubris. I was trained in qualitative research as a graduate student at UCLA. My teachers were the best. Harold Levine, an anthropologist, and Pat McDonough, a sociologist of education, taught the course upon which I closely modeled my class at Temple. As a graduate student I took their course, and then volunteered as a teaching assistant in that class the following year. This experience, and my own thrashing around with my qualitative dissertation for 2 years or so, constituted my "training." While this level of experience is typical for assistant professors, I know that I am now a much more able teacher than I was in those early years. The benefit (in an effort to find a silver lining to my somewhat limited experience) for my students at the time was that I was still very close to the dissertation experience and to the many issues related to becoming a competent qualitative researcher. It is for this reason—that those who have just experienced something often have an easier time describing it to others—that I have collaborated with three of my students on this project. Student chapters are included in this guide, then, as they describe a particular challenge they faced and how they managed in the field. Their novice explorations of these critical topics provide valuable, accessible, relevant insights to students of qualitative research.

Over the years I have become an expert (if I do say so myself) qualitative researcher. I have taught this course many times, overseeing more than 60 short ethnographies. I have conducted several qualitative studies on a variety of topics with varying designs, and I have published in the most selective journals in my field. I have directed several qualitative dissertations and have received funding for my work. My former students have gone on to publish their work in well-regarded, highly selective, peer-reviewed journals.

The course that provides both the foundation and inspiration for this book requires students to do what I think of as mini-ethnographies. Over the 13 weeks of the semester, students learn how to formulate a research question that can be answered by qualitative methods and collect qualitative data through observational and interview techniques. Students enrolled in the course find a site in which to conduct their research; gain access to that site; formulate a research question; collect field notes at the site (this constitutes the major work of the course for the student); conduct interviews with key informants; perform rudimentary data reduction, analysis, and interpretation; and write up their study. The culminating products of the course are a public conference-style poster session where students present their results to their classmates and the broader university community, and a 20-page report of the project that includes some conclusions from the study. It is a notoriously demanding course that requires students to commit to doing at least 6 weeks of fieldwork that will be robust enough for them to write a reasonable report at the end of the semester. It is in the *doing* of this mini-ethnography—developing an answerable question, entering the field, collecting data, and trying to tell a story or answer a question with the data—that students come to understand the basics of the craft.

WHY IS THE PRACTICAL EXPERIENCE
OF DOING RESEARCH SO IMPORTANT?

In my opinion, trying to teach someone how to do qualitative research by telling them about it is like learning about an unknown landscape or region from a guidebook. You can learn something this way. Indeed, if you have a good guidebook or two you can learn a lot. You can effectively plan a trip that includes all the important sites and avoids the hazards. But you will never be able to describe the food eaten by the locals in detail. You will not be able to describe authentically the experience of walking the ground or swimming the seas of a place unless you do it yourself. To really understand a place you need to travel there. Likewise, I have found that the best way to teach students the craft of qualitative research is by having them take a small ethnographic journey. Just like learning to ride a bike, you do not really "get it" until you pedal off on your own and learn (with some astonishment) that speed makes staying upright easier. While I am a strong proponent of taking time to do background research and plan a study, it is not until students are out in the field that they really begin to understand qualitative research.

OVERVIEW OF THE BOOK

The book is designed as a field guide for beginners to qualitative research, and I hope that it will be useful to you as you set off on your own early ethnographic journeys. It is organized into three parts that address the key phases of any ethnographic project: beginning a project, collecting data in the field, and analyzing data and writing about your study. While these discrete phases of qualitative projects are somewhat artificial in that analysis, for instance, is actually part of every phase of a study, they are a useful way to organize learning about qualitative research. I begin every part with a chapter that addresses the critical aspects of each phase of qualitative research and provides my best advice for a beginner. This "how-to" chapter is then paired with a relevant student chapter. The student chapters are based on mini-ethnographies that each student completed with me in my course on qualitative research. They use the language and terms presented in the how-to chapters I have provided. While each student narrative addresses all phases of their research project, from entering the field to writing the 20-page report required for the class, each also emphasizes particular aspects of his or her journey, relating to either beginning, fieldwork, or writing and analysis.

    Part I provides guidance to a novice researcher on starting out. I address site selection and the development of the research question, and suggest useful perspectives and tools to bring on an ethnographic journey. This chapter is paired with the narrative by Mary Lou Heron, a 3rd-year doctoral student. Mary Lou describes her journey through two different research sites as she strove to conduct a meaningful study at a Borders bookstore and café. Her pithy and insightful narrative sheds light on many concerns common to beginners, including finding a site and gaining entry, as well as finding a balance between her own interests and the observable behavior at the site.

Part II addresses fieldwork explicitly. In Chapter 3 I describe how to develop the kind of ethnographic lens that enables a researcher to observe in social settings in a meaningful way. I also address how one goes about collecting data via field notes, observation, and interviews and provide some general "rules of the road" for data collection. This chapter is paired with a chapter by Emily Tancredi-Brice Agbenyega, a 4th-year doctoral student who was both enrolled in my qualitative data course and worked on a funded research project related to her data collection with me. While role management is addressed elsewhere, Emily's ethnographic journey provides a particularly useful reflection on the topic. Her narrative, focused around the idea of positionality, addresses this aspect of fieldwork from the perspective of someone who, as is often the case, had multiple roles at her site and who also managed to collect data as a very busy working mother.

The final section, Part III, explicitly addresses writing and analysis. In Chapter 5 I provide guidance on how to analyze or "make sense" of what you are seeing through various analytic techniques. I also address the role of writing in analysis and provide guidance on the writing process after data collection is concluded. Bradley Bergey, also a graduate student at Temple University, provides the final narrative of the book. His chapter explores the way in which the search for an answerable research question challenged him as he explored why students ask questions in class. His chapter, in particular, highlights the way in which qualitative projects are often like journeys with unexpected twists and turns as he looks for the right question to ask about his interest in students' questions. He delves deeply into the quagmire of deciding which story to tell about his data, providing insights that novice and more seasoned researchers may find useful.

As you learn how to conduct qualitative research, it is as though you are at the start of a journey, and like many travelers to foreign lands you may be both excited and nervous about the unknown terrain that lies ahead. Like other types of travelers, you may have some knowledge of the country to which you are traveling, but this knowledge may be incomplete or imperfect. Traveling is often more fun when you have a companion with whom to share the journey, and better still when your companion has scouted the terrain. We invite you to take this book along as your companion as you learn how to conduct qualitative research.

Acknowledgments

It is a pleasure to be able to thank the many talented and generous people who contributed to the making of this book. Like most other books, the effort that resulted in this volume spanned many years. Along the way there have been several people who have helped me become a better researcher, teacher, and writer. In so doing they contributed to this book.

I am deeply appreciative for the great teaching and mentorship I had during my years at UCLA, where I first learned how to do qualitative research with my own mini-ethnography. My advisor and friend Pat McDonough believed in me and my work early on, held me to a high standard, and spurred me on. Harold Levine taught the original version of the course upon which this book is based—I will always be grateful to him for his wisdom in privileging experience as a teacher and for making me understand the meaning of "it depends."

I have been lucky to have such great students at Temple University. I learn as much from them as I hope they do from me. I am grateful to the students who have taken the qualitative data course with me. It has been a pleasure to be a part of their ethnographic journeys. I am especially grateful to the student collaborators in this book: Bradley Bergey, Emily Tancredi-Brice Agbenyega, and Mary Lou Heron. They took a leap of faith with me by sinking many hours into developing their chapters based on some loose idea for a book I thought we could do together. Our collaboration has been one of the most enjoyable of my career. Thank you for being willing to take the leap, work hard, and be such great colleagues to me and one another.

Many other colleagues supported this work. Most especially I would like to thank my longtime friend and mentor Annette Lareau. Annette has been a fellow traveler and also a guide to me for several years. Her wisdom and kindness are a treasure. My friend and Temple colleague Maia Cucchiara has read every word of this book and provided invaluable advice. It is a great joy to have such a generous colleague, bright scholar, and dear friend so close by, and my work has benefited greatly. Jennifer Cromley, also at Temple, has been a generous and encouraging colleague during the period in which the book was coming together, providing intellectual and financial support that permitted me to undertake this work. I am also grateful to the other colleagues who read the book, especially Temple colleague Catherine Schifter and the anonymous reviewers.

I am deeply indebted to Elizabeth Brach Dyson, who helped at the earliest stages of the book. Talking with her about my ideas for the book and her comments on early drafts helped me to find my voice. She believed in the book from the start. Without her editorial wisdom and encouragement, I am certain it never would have been written. I hope I will someday have another project for us to work on. Brian Ellerbeck at Teachers College Press has been a pleasure to work with. I am grateful for his able support and good advice in bringing this book to publication.

I would also like to thank my family and friends for their support—most especially my two daughters, Margaret and Kate, who listened patiently to me throughout the process of writing this book and lived with all of the ups and downs it occasioned, all the while encouraging me along. I am particularly indebted to Margaret for her smart suggestion for the title. My deepest thanks of all go to my husband, Paul, who makes my work and life as I know it possible.

Part I

BEGINNING

CHAPTER ONE

Thoughts for the Uninitiated on Starting a Qualitative Project

Erin Horvat

Often when students begin their first foray into qualitative research they are full of questions. This chapter is designed to answer many of the most common questions and provide insight to students who are just starting out on an ethnographic journey.

WHAT IS QUALITATIVE RESEARCH? WHAT IS ETHNOGRAPHY?

What is the difference between an ethnography and qualitative research? This is a good question to start with. The qualitative paradigm contains many different modes of inquiry, and the terms *ethnography, ethnomethodology, symbolic interactionism,* and *qualitative research* are often used interchangeably and without precise definitions. Novice researchers are often puzzled by these terms as they struggle to determine what kind of research they want to do. A full explanation of these various approaches is not possible or appropriate here. I will, however, offer a few words on the topic that may be helpful to beginning researchers.

I find it useful to think of qualitative research as an umbrella that provides the basic epistemological assumptions that guide the paradigm. So, what is epistemology and what is the qualitative epistemological stance? Briefly, epistemology is the study of knowledge. The *Stanford Encyclopedia of Philosophy* defines *epistemology* as "the study of knowledge and justified belief" (http://plato.stanford.edu/entries/epistemology/). This branch of philosophy explores what is knowledge, how it is acquired, and how we know what we know. It is also concerned with the standards for justifying how we know what we know. So, as a researcher your epistemological stance refers to the way you believe or justify that belief that you "know" something based on your research. Methodological epistemology can be thought of as determining how we convince others that we know something. These are the standards by which we judge the validity and reliability of the knowledge generated by a research study. Different methodological traditions have different standards by which validity and reliability are evaluated.

Qualitative research lies within the interpretivist paradigm. The interpretivist tradition, broadly conceived, is concerned with the understanding and unmasking of the meaning that individuals assign to their actions in a social setting. In direct contrast to positivist epistemology, interpretivist researchers are not interested in testing hypotheses and do not believe in a single objective truth. Rather, they are interested in understanding the meaning or "truths" of a particular social world.

Often, though not always, this means that research questions shift and change over time as the researcher comes to a more fully developed understanding of the social space and the actions of actors in it. Thus, rather than formulating a formal unchangeable research question or testing hypotheses (as is the norm in positivist epistemology), qualitative researchers more often than not begin a study by selecting the people, process, or place they want to study rather than a formal question. Over time, as they learn more about the focus of their study, a research question emerges. Sometimes, after a researcher has spent a good deal of time and energy in an area or can draw on the work of others on a particular topic, a qualitative researcher will enter the field with a formal research question that does not change over time. I have found this to be rare. When I enter a project with a research question, more often than not that question is changed or amended before the end of the study.

As almost all texts on qualitative research point out, the approach is best suited to addressing "how" and "why" questions as opposed to "how much" or "how many" questions. Usually qualitative researchers are interested in the meaning behind actions in a social context. They see value in providing an in-depth understanding of social worlds.

Ethnography is a way of doing research that lies within the interpretivist methodological paradigm. It is primarily focused on the relationship between action in a social setting and the culture or context of that setting. The word *ethnography*, from the Greek, is drawn from the words *ethnos*, which means folk or people, and *grapho*, which means to write. An ethnography, then, is a written document that seeks to describe the nature of a people. The notion of ethnography as a research methodology has expanded somewhat over time; today's ethnographies sometimes include pictures or video, and our definitions of "a people" are more varied. While in the early 20th century ethnographies were often conducted on populations foreign to oneself, such as Bronislaw Malinowski's studies of Papua New Guineans in 1914 or William Foote Whyte's study of Cornerville in his 1943 publication of *Street Corner Society* (1943/1993), ethnographies have more recently expanded to include studies of other less culturally or geographically bounded groups of people, such as Peter Bearman's 2005 study of New York City doormen or Mitchell Duneier's study of the regular patrons at a Chicago cafeteria.

Most ethnographies are usually situated in a specific time and place. They generally also seek to understand the nature of a group of people, process, or place. There are some qualitative studies that are not ethnographies. I think of such studies—those that employ participant observation and interview, or focus groups, or case-study approaches that are not fundamentally interested in the culture of a place or people—as qualitative studies that are *not* ethnographies, even though they may use some of the methods usually associated with ethnography.

WHY DO A QUALITATIVE STUDY?

Often students come to me when they are just beginning to think about the kind of research they want to do. In many cases, students arrive at my door knowing that they are interested in questions that they do not think can be answered by statistical analyses. They are also usually interested in interacting with people in order to answer their research question. Sometimes they are afraid of the math required for sophisticated statistical analyses and conclude therefore that they are more well-suited to qualitative research. They often say, "I am just a qualitative person." Some students think that qualitative research will be easier than quantitative, although usually they are smart enough not to come right out and say so. Often students are driven by all of these factors, as well as a romanticized image of ethnography.

My first step is usually to disabuse students of the idea that a qualitative study will be "easier" than a quantitative one. Good qualitative work takes time, and lots of it. As I outline further in Chapter 3, there is often a direct relationship between the amount and quality of the time spent at the site of the study and the quality of the study itself. In order to understand the people, place, or process you are studying, you need to spend time with them. And while complex statistical techniques may not be central to your analysis, qualitative researchers often struggle with other equally daunting challenges, such as keeping up with the field notes from their study, clarifying and remaining focused on the objectives of their work, exploring the theoretical foundations and implications of their work, and managing their role at the research site. All of these aspects of qualitative work will be addressed in further detail. However, I raise them here simply to note that high-quality qualitative work is no less rigorous or demanding than its cousin, high-quality quantitative work. The most critical difference between the two is the epistemological assumptions that guide the research enterprise, not the ease of the approach.

Fear of math is not a reason to conduct a qualitative study. Interest in people, how they make sense of their world, and what processes occur in a particular context is. Ultimately the kind of study that emerges, the actual design of the study, and the decisions that the researcher makes in the field will be driven by the research question. Often, however, the question itself is less than clear at the start of a study. So when should one consider conducting a qualitative study?

Usually students know they are interested in studying a particular population, process, or place. My students have studied many interesting *populations*, such as adolescent readers, high school students in detention, wheelchair rugby players, patrons of an African hair-braiding salon, teachers in a special education classroom, or youth at a mall. Students have also been interested in studying particular *processes*, such as how high school students pick colleges to apply to, how students decide whether or not to ask a question in class, how varsity college coaches get the attention of their athletes in practice and communicate with them, or how teachers in an elementary school use technology. Often students are interested in studying a particular *place*. Frequently, these places are chosen because the student believes he or she might see something relating to a particular population, process, or question of interest to her or him, but the study begins as a study of the place. For example, former students of mine have studied bookstores, libraries, a coffee shop, a nonprofit organization promoting AIDS awareness, and an innovative program for low-income adults working toward an associate's degree.

Some researchers, usually those with experience in and knowledge of the field or area of inquiry, enter the field with a firm notion of their research focus. Others know only that they are interested in a particular site and want to see what happens there. In addition, as Bradley Bergey highlights in Chapter 6, research questions develop over time as a part of the research process. Usually students who are new to qualitative research have a relatively vague idea of their research question, since they are new to the field and have not had a chance to do pilot research to test out ideas. In all cases, however, qualitative studies are aimed at understanding the situated meaning of actions and processes.

QUALITATIVE RESEARCH: WHAT IS IT GOOD FOR?

As I note in the Preface to this volume, there have been many times when I have had to defend qualitative research as a reasonable way to learn something. While part of this need to justify or defend qualitative research is a product of a lack of understanding of the approach and the quite highly developed methodological standards that govern it, it is also a product of the results-oriented society in which we live.

We live in a results-oriented society focused on "measurable outcomes." Particularly in the field of education, politicians, policymakers, and practitioners are looking for "what works." We are desperate to find the solution or solutions that will "solve the problem of our schools." It is true that there is room for improvement in American education. For instance, we rank 21st overall when compared with other industrialized nations in the 2009 Programme for International Student Assessment (PISA) combined results. According to our own 2011 National Assessment of Educational Progress (NAEP), 65% of 8th-graders cannot read or do math at a proficient level. Many reasonable people, including parents, politicians, and policymakers, would like to see us do better. For example, as Mary Lou Heron notes in her chapter, she, like many others trying to solve this problem, want to be able to say that "65% of students see an improvement in reading ability" with a specific intervention. Specific percentages or tests of significance can be appealing, not only to policymakers, but to wider audiences as well, as they convey authority, suggest generalizability, and are easily and quickly quoted. Our search for solutions to many policy problems seems tailor-made for quantitative studies. If we want to be able to say that we are seeing gains in measurable achievement, we need to be able to measure the gains made by an educational intervention among our students. Our policy conversation is thus centered on "how much" and "how many" questions: How much achievement for how many kids through what intervention? Quantitative methods are useful in responding to these questions. These analyses are most useful for testing hypotheses and interventions, and tend to suggest generalizability.

We are also interested in finding solutions to this problem that will work for a lot of kids. Generally, the Department of Education is not going to be interested in an intervention or approach that only works well in a specific context. Policymakers are rightly interested in scalability. Something has been shown to work in a single school? Great, is it "scalable?" That means, while it is nice that one K–8 school in Philadelphia got great results on standardized tests after intensive training for parents on how to help their kids with homework, for example, the intervention is not useful from the perspective of policymakers unless it is "scalable." The "silver bullet" or intervention needs to be something that can be implemented in a wide range of schools with limited budgets. Qualitative research is in large part contextually bound. The method is well suited to studying specific definable contexts or people or processes, and what we learn may or may not be transferable to a different context and may or may not be "scalable."[1]

So, given this policy context that focuses on measurable outcomes and scalable interventions and the limitations inherent in most qualitative work, what role is there for qualitative research? What is it good for in the current policy or research context? Most textbooks on qualitative methods note that qualitative research is most useful in understanding processes (as opposed to outcomes, per se) and, as I detail below, is particularly useful when little is already known about a particular topic. It is also well suited to understanding a part of our social world from an insider or emic perspective and building theory based on these new perspectives.

Qualitative research is particularly well suited to the describing and understanding of processes or problems. Once we have this understanding, we can begin to build theories related to the roots of the problem or to devise solutions to the problem. Often we do not have any idea how to solve a problem because we really do not understand the problem in the first place. Before we go around tossing out solutions to the problem, it is best to gain a deep and comprehensive understanding of the problem and its origins. This is one of the places where qualitative research can be really valuable.

The story of the development of the Swiffer in Jonah Lerher's book *Imagine: How Creativity Works* (2012) provides an excellent example. As Lerher reports, Proctor and Gamble had a problem. They were desperately looking for a way to develop new household cleaning products. However, after years of failed efforts by chemists to develop new and better soaps, the company turned to a design firm to help them develop new products.

The company's designers did not begin by immediately developing new soaps. Rather, they began by watching people. Focusing on floor cleaning, they watched, took field notes, and videotaped real people cleaning floors in their homes. They watched person after person dip or plunge an unwieldy mop into a bucket or tub of water that became progressively dirtier and wipe it on the floor. Through these hours of observation they were able to understand the problem of floor cleaning. What they learned was that what people needed to get their floors clean were not necessarily better soaps but, rather, a better mop. Observation about the *qualitative* nature of people's actions allowed the researchers to understand and reframe the problem of floor cleaning. Only after developing this better understanding of the problem were they able to design a solution. As a result, now, rather than dipping a marginally clean stringy mop into dirty water to clean their floors, millions of Americans buy Swiffer disposable sheets that attach to the patented Swiffer device to clean their floors. Describing and understanding a problem is often a necessary first step to devising a solution, and qualitative research is especially well suited to this type of enterprise. And for Proctor and Gamble, understanding the problem allowed them to reframe it and design a solution that led to over $500 million in profits in the first year alone.

What, if anything, does the Swiffer have to do with educational or social science research? A great deal, it turns out. In almost every endeavor it is best to understand a problem before we begin designing solutions. An example I learned about from one of my students who has done extensive service learning work in Nicaragua makes this point. My student, Nora Reynolds, developed a nonprofit organization called Water for Waslala, which provides clean water for remote communities. Her dissertation research explores the impact of U.S. service learning programs on the communities in which they are working. Often there are unintended consequences of these projects. She relayed one telling incident from the Water for Waslala Blog (http://waterforwaslala.wordpress.com/2012/08/29/why-do-development-projects-fail-stories-about-the-importance-of-working-with). In one town, optometrists had traveled to a rural village to conduct vision consultations. Due to limited resources, they used Bibles to conduct vision tests. When they asked the villagers if they could read the Bible they answered "No." So the optometrists provided reading glasses for the villagers. The people could certainly see better, but they still could not read because they were illiterate. Rather than understanding that the villagers could not read, they assumed they understood the problem and erroneously thought the villagers could not see. Taking time to understand and describe a problem or process is an important epistemological first step.

Most qualitative studies also share a focus on problems of processes *in context*. The Swiffer designers did not bring people into a lab and provide them with cleaning tools and ask them to clean, they watched them *in their homes*. This is another, often defining feature and strength of qualitative work: the research occurs in the lived context and is framed from the perspective of those in the context—the emic perspective. Another example from closer to home, which illustrates both the way in which qualitative research is well suited to providing an in-depth understanding of a process and the importance of social context, is Michelle Fine's 1991 study *Framing Dropouts*.

In this ethnographic work, Fine sought to understand a problem, high school dropout rates, which, by her own account, had received scant attention at the time. She asked: "If public education is indeed accessible to all, how is it that most low-income urban youths attending comprehensive high schools fail to graduate?" (1991, p. 8). After surveying the literature and finding very little on high school dropouts, Fine situated her inquiry in one comprehensive high school and framed the problem as one of process. She endeavored to "study the making of dropouts" (p. 5). Her research reframed the "problem" of dropouts. Rather than focusing on only the students themselves, she focused on the institutions that produced such high rates of dropout and the "institutional policies and practices that enable, obscure, and legitimate" dropout rates of 40% to 60% for urban youth. While silver-bullet solutions to the problem of school dropout did not result from the research, *Framing Dropouts* reconceptualized the problem. This reframing and better understanding of the problem, which can then lead to well-designed solutions and the building of theories to explain high dropout rates, was possible only because the research was situated in context and focused on process rather than outcome.

Often, we make the same mistake in public or educational policy as the optometrists in the previous example. We either assume we understand the problem and devise a solution, or we do not bother to try to understand the problem in all of its complexity in social context before designing a solution. In reality, the world and schools are very complex places. Children come to schools with myriad approaches to learning and cultural backgrounds that impact their education. Our interventions have a much better chance of working if we can spend time describing and understanding the problem of poor achievement from the perspective of the lived context before we throw solutions at it. Qualitative research is well suited to defining and describing problems and processes from an emic perspective that is rooted in social context.

WHAT IS A GOOD QUESTION FOR A QUALITATIVE STUDY?

While it is helpful to tell students who are interested in qualitative research that the approach is best suited to how and why questions and that qualitative researchers are usually interested in the meaning behind events in social settings, this direction can seem rather vague and opaque to students who are just starting out. In other words, it is often not very helpful. I have found that while I can spend time talking with students in the abstract about what makes for a good question, it is not until they work to formulate their own question and collect data to answer it that they begin to understand how questions are developed. It is in the field that students begin to understand how questions are derived; how questions develop over time at the site; and, in most cases, that they are the product of their own interest, insights from theory or literature, and the practical ability to answer the questions (e.g., time, money, access).

In my experience students come to the study of qualitative research and the opportunity to conduct their first small study at many places along what I think of as the "question continuum." Some students have spent a significant amount of time immersed in the literature of a particular field and arrive with well-formed questions. They have spent time reading in a particular substantive area and have an understanding of the questions that have been posed already in the field and what questions are ripe for further exploration. Some students come with very specific well-developed questions based on this exploration of the literature. Others come to the class with no very specific question at all but rather a desire to learn the skills associated with the craft. It is perfectly fine for students to start out as learners at any point on this continuum. More advanced researchers are often well advised to position themselves along the more well-informed points along this continuum by situating their interest or question in the literature and developing a well-articulated theoretical position or stance, but for beginners, this is less important. Wherever one lies on this continuum, questions are usually informed by the researcher's curiosity, the ability of the researcher to answer a particular question, and the insights gleaned from ongoing data collection and analysis.

One of the more surprising aspects of the process of conducting their first qualitative project for students is the degree of flexibility regarding the research question. As students spend time in the field and slowly come to understand what they may be able to learn at their site, they usually realize that they will need to change their research question. This is surprising to them. "You mean I can change my research question?" Yes, Virginia, you can change your research question. It is a work in progress. Unlike the deductive quantitative approach where a specific hypothesis is being tested, qualitative research is more exploratory and inductive in nature. Accordingly, our questions shift and change as we learn in the field, as we discover and explore the people, place, or process of interest to us and understand the meaning of actions in a particular social context. Many students do not settle on the exact question they will answer in their report until they write the first draft, as they discover the meaning behind their data through the writing. I think that because most learning about scientific inquiry is modeled on the positivistic assumptions that underlie quantitative research, the flexible and shifting nature of this approach takes some getting used to for most people. All this ambiguity and change can make some people very uncomfortable. However, it is the nature of the approach that questions can emerge from the data being collected, and they can change over time.

WHAT MAKES FOR A GOOD SITE
WHEN STARTING A QUALITATIVE PROJECT?

What should you look for when you are thinking about locating a possible site to collect qualitative data? The first prerequisite is that you are curious about what you might see at any given site. You will be spending a good bit of time at this site and so it is helpful if it is a place you find interesting. A genuine sense of curiosity about this place and people or process you might observe is a prerequisite. This is followed closely by a sufficient level of observable activity, reasonable boundaries, and the ability to gain access to the site and collect data there.

As Mary Lou Heron describes in detail in Chapter 2, the site needs to have enough activity. Generally speaking, a site where not much is going on, where you will not see interaction among individuals, is best avoided. The site must also be a place that has an identifiable boundary. While the boundaries of the research site may shift over the course of a study as the researcher gets to know the site and the research question evolves, it is important to be able to identify some boundaries of the site. The boundaries help the researcher to determine what to watch and write down, what "counts" as data. Without boundaries or with boundaries that are too loosely defined, the researcher, especially novice researchers, can have a hard time settling on a focus at the site.

It can be a good idea to take a brief field trip to the site before you collect data. What kind of activity do you see? Are people talking? Interacting? Do you think you would like to spend a significant amount of time here? Sometimes people imagine or suppose that a place will be interesting and then find that it is not. One of my students observed at a food court at a mall. While he was interested in observing the patrons and anticipated that there would be a continual flow of people ordering food and eating in the seating area, there was not. He wound up watching the same eight people sip coffee for six weeks. As Mary Lou Heron describes, she was interested in the library at a nearby college. Unfortunately, while the structure itself was stately and beautiful, and one would reasonably expect that students would use the facility, they did not. She wound up changing sites in order to find a place with enough people in it.

Ethnographers have studied neighborhoods, companies, schools, and classrooms. They have studied small groups of people (three to four) as well as larger groups. These studies all vary in scope. They also vary in the length of time it took to complete them. Beginners need to start with projects that are reasonable in scale and scope and that have relatively firm boundaries. For example, if you are interested in the way that children use playground space you could design a project at a single school where you observe the playground. But what if this school has different playgrounds for older and younger kids? What if it is used during the day by kids at the school and in the afternoons by members from the surrounding community? How do you define your site under these conditions? Do you observe before, during, and after school? Do you spend time at all of the different playground sites? How do you decide where to observe and for how long? It depends on how you define the boundaries of your site in addition to your research question, and what you can possibly manage to observe.

You will need to draw some distinct boundaries. Rather than thinking about your project as one that investigates how children use playground space, your project could become defined as one that investigates how children in grades 1 through 3 use a climbing structure at a school playground. What does this mean for your definition of the site? Instead of the site being the whole playground it is now restricted to the climbing structure. You are also now more interested in younger children who attend school there, so you will be observing primarily during recess. Both the figurative and literal boundaries of your site are more clearly defined.

In addition to finding a site that is interesting to you, that has enough activity, and can be appropriately bounded, you must be able to gain access to the site. Usually this means that someone at the site must give you written or verbal permission to observe. It also means that you must be able to observe at the site when there is activity and when you have been granted access to be there. As I detail later it is better to make your case to observe at a place in person. It is also important that you are able to observe at the site at a time when interaction is occurring. You may have an interest in kindergarten parents and how they connect with one another and the school when their kids begin to go to school. It may be ideal to observe the process of how kindergarten parents pick up and drop off their children at school. Do they hang out in the schoolyard? Talk to the teacher? Do parents connect with one another? These are all activities you might be able to observe. But you would have to go to the school almost every day to observe for two brief periods of time of maybe half an hour each, once at dropoff and once at pickup each day. Is it reasonable for you to think you will be able to be at the school every day on that schedule? While the principal may have approved your study and granted you access, your own schedule may not permit you access to the relevant activity.

So remember: the best research sites need to have a sufficient level of activity, be accessible to you, and, above all, interest you.

WHAT DO I NEED TO BRING TO MY SITE?

I like to be a smart packer. I hate taking too much stuff that I wind up dragging around on a trip but do not use. But I really get my nose out of joint if I do not have something I should have known to bring with me on a trip. I like having the right stuff, so I pay careful attention to what I pack. As you pack for your qualitative journey there are a few essentials you do not want to be without. Like a good raincoat or travel pillow, you can probably get through the trip without these items, but I would not recommend it.

A High Tolerance for Ambiguity

Pat McDonough, one of my research mentors, talked about the need to have a "high tolerance for ambiguity" when doing qualitative work. Ambiguity refers to a sense of uncertainty, of indefiniteness. Why would one need a high tolerance for uncertainty or lack of clarity in learning ethnography? Why indeed. While it may sound trite, change and uncertainty are really the only constants in the field. It is easy to feel like you really do not know where you are headed on your journey, when you might get there, or even why you are going on the trip. This is normal. Most students of ethnography begin their inquiry with a general idea of what they might like to learn something about. They pick a site where they might be likely to see interactions among individuals that bear on their research interest. However, this is a shot in the dark in many respects.

Plan though we might, the real world is a messy place. Often we do not see the kinds of interactions we hope and could reasonably expect to see in a given site. One student from my class provides a case in point. Jenny[2] was interested in observing at a school that was rolling out a new program using iPads and, as she stated in her Site Selection Prospectus, her interest revolved around "teachers and trying to facilitate their 'buy-in' to using technology." She had ideas based on many years of teaching and her extensive reading of the literature about barriers to technology use for teachers. She found a school that had technology in the classrooms and that was enthusiastic about having her come and spend some time with them. However, when she started observing she realized that while she was able to observe what teachers did and how they used technology, getting at the barriers to technology use was harder than she had anticipated. Often the barriers were not observable. Frequently, the barriers were beliefs about technology or teaching that were embedded in teachers' practices. Observing these beliefs turned out to be too difficult. However, as she began observing at her site Jenny noticed how *students* facilitated technology use. Consequently, Jenny changed her research question to one that allowed her to explore how students facilitated teacher technology use. While ultimately the shift in her research question resulted in a good study, it took time for the question to emerge and the whole process made Jenny a little uncomfortable. She was able to turn in a very nice study by shifting her research focus onto aspects of teaching and technology that could be observed at her site. She also learned a great deal about what she will need to do to conduct a study investigating her original question.

Jenny's experience is not unusual. In a recent study I conducted with my colleague Maia Cucchiara, we set out to understand why middle-class parents would choose to send their children to an urban public school.[3] We were interested in their motivations. Our study was focused on interviews with parents in a particular urban public school community. As the research progressed, however, we began to understand that not only did we need to talk to parents who had chosen that urban public school, we also needed to talk with parents who had made other choices. We needed to broaden our understanding of what it meant to choose and needed to talk with people who had made the choice that interested us as well as those who had made a different choice. Thus we changed our data collection strategy to include parents who could have selected this school but chose an independent or charter school. More often than not, the research question and the data collection strategy are adjusted over the course of a study. It is critical to be able to be open to these changes and tolerate the ambiguity they bring to the project.

Likewise, qualitative studies often raise unexpected or unanticipated questions or findings. While the uncertainty this brings to a study can be disconcerting, it is, in fact, one of the great strengths of the approach. An example from my own research with James Davis may be useful.[4] James and I were engaged in a study of graduates from YouthBuild, a program with many sites all over the country that provides job training, life skills assistance, and education to high school dropouts. Working with YouthBuild staff and other quantitative researchers, we had designed a mixed-methods study aimed at understanding the impact the program had made on graduates lives. We had spent considerable time developing the interview protocol we would use, testing it out on a sample of graduates and revising it based on their feedback as well as that of staff and other researchers. However, it was not until we were out in the field that we hit upon a critical question that was missing from the protocol.

One young man we interviewed at our first site visit was describing his life prior to entering the program. In his description he said he did not think he would live to be very old if it were not for the program—that the program had, in effect, saved his life. When he said, "So I only thought I'd live to be nineteen. I'm serious. I had people come over on my twenty-first birthday just to shake my hand and say, 'I didn't think you'd make it this far,'" we realized that we had uncovered something important. As we asked him why he did not think he would live past 19 and how YouthBuild had changed his life expectancy, an important story about the power of this program was revealed. The original interview protocol had asked questions about other anticipated outcomes from the program, such as better employment prospects, reduction in drug use, et cetera. However, we had not considered that the program could affect something as fundamental and important as life expectancy. Our interview protocol was amended to specifically ask every graduate how old they thought they would live to be prior to YouthBuild and then again following the program completion. In the end, this question yielded some of the most telling and important findings in the study. We were also able to add a question regarding life expectancy to the quantitative survey that followed our exploratory qualitative work. The unexpected ability of the program to alter a student's life expectancy was a significant and powerful finding of the study. The ability to remain open to the indefiniteness and contingent nature of the research enterprise was critical in uncovering this finding.

Qualitative research is rife with ambiguity. Research questions evolve. Interview protocols are adjusted and plans for data collection change. I think of it as a contingent science. What you are looking for and how you look for it changes according to the demands of the field. This makes some people very uncomfortable, while others revel in the freedom to adjust. Whether you come to it naturally or need to work to achieve it, it is wise to pack a high tolerance for ambiguity in your suitcase.

The Ability to Laugh at Oneself

Like most experiences in life, the process of conducting qualitative research is enhanced by the ability to laugh (often at oneself), to not take oneself too seriously and to maintain a sense of adventure and excitement about the project. Unlike other modes of inquiry, qualitative research requires these "soft skills." Because the researcher is the instrument of data collection—the words and actions are recorded by the researcher and study participants are interviewed by the researcher—the way in which the researcher interacts with her environment influences the project.

Being able to laugh at oneself often helps researchers while collecting data by allowing them to connect with the participants at their site. Daily life is often full of humorous events, which provide an opportunity to connect with others at the site. My colleague Maia Cucchiara recollected serving red water ice (a type of red Italian ice similar to a snow cone) at a school fair, where she observed and shared a laugh with a parent volunteer over the red sticky mess their hands and arms had become over the course of the afternoon. Rather than grumpily lamenting the fact that she was up to her elbows in sticky red water ice and questioning the value of this activity as a part of her study, Maia was able to find the humor in her circumstance and use it to connect with a study participant. Laughing together with this parent provided a point of connection. Similarly, there have been many times when, in my research in schools, I have laughed with a parent or teacher participant over some playground mishap. This shared moment often opened up an opportunity to talk with the participant at that moment or later in the study.

It is also important to be able to laugh at the mistakes you will make in the field. There is no perfect study. Mistakes and misunderstandings happen. Being able to laugh at them and learn from them is an important skill in fieldwork. In one recent study my colleagues and I were trying to recruit middle-class families from one school to our study. We had developed a sign and a lovely one-page handout about the study and set up a table during back-to-school night to recruit parents. Based on demographic data we had previously collected about the school, we had reason to believe that more than half of the families would fall into the middle-class category. However, as parents talked to us they repeatedly insisted that they could not participate because they were not middle class. To our amazement, they thought they were working class. Despite the fact that their incomes and jobs would have placed them firmly in the middle class according to our definition, they did not see themselves as middle class. It would have been easy to be upset about this turn of events. We had missed an important recruitment opportunity. We had misread the attitudes of the parents we wanted to study. However, rather than beating ourselves up about it, it was more effective to laugh about it and take away a lesson about recruiting parents to such a study. Rather than assuming that we and our potential participants would have similar concepts of class status, we learned that a better approach was to gain participation and then, after the initial contact, discuss employment status and other class markers rather than use a global designation of working-class or middle-class status. Based on this experience we revised our recruitment materials and went on to successfully solicit parents' participation in the study. Maintaining a positive attitude that allows you to laugh at and learn from your mistakes can help your fieldwork.

A Sense of Humility

In some ways the act of doing research is quite selfish, or at least self-directed. The researcher gets to decide what question is worth pursuing and how best to pursue it. Ultimately we get to decide what claims to make based on our work. We also rightly get the blame when the project goes badly.

Due to the self-directed nature of the work, as we conduct research our focus shifts. Rather than putting family, or teaching, or at times our own health first (Been to the gym lately? Can't get that doctor's appointment scheduled?), we tend to prioritize our research. Those important people around us (spouses, significant others, students, children) know that when we are consumed by our project we can become quite selfish as our calendar becomes dominated by events requiring our presence at the research site rather than our routine activities. We may not make it to important family events; we may shirk our share of household duties.

While all of this makes doing research somewhat perilous for healthy relationships and work–life balance, it can also affect our own sense of place in the world. Given that we get to make all of these critical decisions and prioritize our work, it is not a stretch to begin to believe our own press, so to speak. It can be easy to begin to think that *we* are the critical important figures in the research. Nothing could be further from the truth. Recognizing this and working to maintain a sense of humility and gratitude for the privilege of being allowed into people's lives and for the support and tolerance of family, friends, and colleagues is crucial. While qualitative research requires much of you as a person, it is not *about* you. Maintaining a healthy sense of humility will prevent you from sliding down this slippery slope of overblown self-importance.

A Sense of Adventure

Like most journeys, this one will be more fun and probably go more smoothly if you maintain a sense of adventure. This sense of adventure includes an excitement about where you are going, a sense of openness to what you find on your trip, and a "can-do" flexible attitude that propels you toward your destination despite setbacks. Adventurers often improvise solutions to problems. Rather than giving up on the trip or trek and heading home when equipment breaks or a bridge is washed out, real adventurers repair equipment and find alternate routes to their destination. Likewise, qualitative researchers improvise solutions to problems in the field. They are undaunted by initial refusals of access to research sites; they have backup equipment and adjust to changes in the data collection plan. Packing a sense of adventure keeps your enthusiasm high in the face of long hours of tedious work and helps you to remain undeterred by challenges that inevitably litter the territory.

Reasonable Expectations

Sometimes it can be helpful to have wildly unrealistic deadlines. At times, especially at work, I am a fan of this approach. I am deadline-sensitive. Most things in my life happen right before they need to. Books are returned to the library the night they are due, papers get graded by the time grades need to be turned in, not before, and a deadline is essential to getting writing done. Could I possibly grade 20 graduate-level 20-page papers in a single day? Can I write a book chapter in a weekend? The answer is usually "no." But what does happen is that I get a very good start on these projects as a result of the unrealistic deadlines. However, I have the benefit of years of experience doing this work and have a handle on what might be possible or impossible.

Beginning students of qualitative research rarely have this experience. They often unknowingly set unrealistic deadlines and expectations.

Often, as students begin my course I have to let them know that they will, in fact, not be able to unlock the mystery of the achievement gap in 13 weeks. Usually, once I restate to the student what they have told me they want to do and ask them if they think they can reasonably answer the question they have posed in the time allotted, they grin sheepishly and begin the process of scaling back and paring down the question to a manageable scope and size. As Bradley Bergey notes in Chapter 6, this pruning takes time—sometimes the whole semester. As students prune their questions they begin to understand the relationship between the research question, the time they will have to collect data, and the claims they may make.

As students begin to understand that some of their expectations for their mini-ethnography are unreasonable, they begin to establish *reasonable* expectations. Research questions become focused on observable phenomena. Research sites become places where one would actually see people interacting. Possible claims become more concrete, modest, and observable. In short, the project becomes something that could be carried out in the time allowed.

Packing some reasonable expectations and leaving your unrealistic ones at home is a good idea as you set out on your journey. Despite the fact that unrealistic expectations sound better when we tell people about our studies (I really am engaged in important work! I am going to fix X problem!) and the fact that some of us are motivated by wildly unrealistic expectations, reasonable expectations will actually be more useful to you on your trip. Starting out, it is a good idea to ask what, on the face of it, is an answerable question. It is good to be very realistic with yourself about the amount of time and energy you can devote to the project. While it may sound good at the beginning to say you will visit your site every day, this is usually an unrealistic expectation. Keeping up with the field notes alone would prevent such a strategy. And while it might be useful to hope that your project could be a published paper, this too is unrealistic for a study of the size and scope one can usually carry out in the length of one semester. The same logic extends to theses, dissertations, and other research projects. While you may have more time, it is not unlimited. There are limits to what you can accomplish within a year or several-months-long project. Being realistic about these expectations will allow you to design a high-quality project that you actually finish.

Respect for Descriptive Studies

Oftentimes students feel enormous pressure to *show* something. They want to be able to *show* that teacher expectations influence student performance. They want to *show* that peers influence college destinations of high school seniors. Usually these are very difficult things to show. While it may be true that teacher expectations influence student performance or that peers do influence high school seniors' college destinations, actually designing a qualitative study that shows this relationship is easier said than done. As noted earlier, qualitative research is best suited to questions that explore meaning and process. These types of questions are typically why and how questions. Often they are answered by "simply" describing a phenomenon or process. So while it may not be possible to show that teachers' expectations influence students' performance, it might be possible to conduct a small study describing teacher expectations in a classroom and interview students regarding their understanding of these expectations. You could describe the two sides of this relationship. Showing that one part of the relationship causes the other is a much more difficult thing.[5]

Once students understand the difficulty of conducting research that can *show* something definitively, they can be quite dismayed. They often fear that their work will not be important or worthy if it does not show something—if it cannot make causal claims. It is at this juncture that it is useful to point out that some of the most important work done in the social sciences has been descriptive in nature. I often point out that Jean Piaget,[6] the renowned developmental psychologist who is best known for his work documenting the emotional and cognitive development of children, and Elisabeth Kubler-Ross, the psychiatrist who documented the five stages of death and dying in her book *On Death and Dying* (1997), simply described human processes. Both of these groundbreaking researchers used naturalistic observation and interview to describe and provide an analytic framework for a commonly observed process. Neither Kubler-Ross nor Piaget linked one variable with another. Kubler-Ross did not show that dying people all go through a certain process. Rather, she described in great detail the way in which more than 500 people she interviewed and observed coped with the grief of a terminal illness or tragedy. Similarly, Piaget did not "discover" that children developed. Rather, he described, in rich analytical detail, the stages of child development as he understood them from his research. Thus important work can be done by "just" describing what we see. The trick of course is to describe it in a meaningful way that uncovers an important "truth" about a phenomenon of consequence.

Bread for the Journey

It is also important to sustain oneself on a journey of discovery. Bread for the Journey is a remarkable a nonprofit organization that "give[s] small, timely grants to social entrepreneurs in their communities. These grassroots micro-grants help jump-start valuable projects aimed at making their communities more vital, healthy, and just" (www.breadforthejourney.org). The idea behind these grants is to provide "bread," basic fundamental nutrition, to people on their journey to nourish, support, and sustain the work.

Similar to the entrepreneurial journeys engaged in by grantees of Bread for the Journey, qualitative researchers need to find what nourishes them on their qualitative journey and pack it in their suitcase. This nourishment can literally be food. Often while collecting data regular mealtimes fly by. Having what I often refer to as "emergency food" (granola bars, a piece of fruit, etc.) with you can mean the difference between capturing an important event and missing it while you are searching for lunch. This nourishment can be relationships with colleagues. It is often lonely to collect data. While you will spend much of your time collecting data in the company of other people, you will not be able to interact in a free and authentic way with them, as they are participants in your study. You will be watching and taking notes. It may not be appropriate to talk with them about what you are finding as you watch them or to share aspects of your personal life with them. Developing and maintaining strong relationships with colleagues who can understand your work and in whom you can confide can nourish and sustain you. Making sure you tend to your intimate relationships (significant other, children, parents) is critical as well, as they can nourish you during this journey. Your task is to determine what you need to remain strong, focused, and engaged as you complete your work and then go about creating those supports for yourself.

Tools of the Trade

In addition to these items you will need to pack what I think of as the tools of the trade: a notebook, a couple of pens, an audio recorder, perhaps a GPS device, and a map. While I provide more detail on writing field notes in Chapter 3, I list here the basic "kit" of tools you will want to have with you when you head out into the field. When you go into the field you will need a way to record what it is you are seeing. I usually do this on a small notepad. Recently, I discovered "reporter's notebooks," which are 4" x 8" in size and contain ruled notepaper. For me this notebook is just the right size. It is not so big (like an 8.5" x 11" pad) that it can be hard to write on while standing up and it is not too small to contain my unruly scrawl. It also has a cover that can be flipped down in order to cover your notes. You should use whatever size you are comfortable with. Even if I am bringing a laptop[7] to the field with me, I like to have a notepad. I never know if I will be more comfortable typing notes or writing them. I also want to be prepared to be able to get up and follow the study participants if they begin walking around. Having a notebook allows me to do that.

I also usually carry an audio recorder with me as well as extra batteries. They are small and easy to carry. While I do not always audio-record impromptu informal interviews that may occur in the field, I want to be prepared to do so should the need arise. Having the recorder with me allows me to exercise the option of recording a conversation.

I also usually make sure my car has a GPS device and a good map, especially if it is my first time going to the site or if I am meeting a participant for an interview. Even though I may know how to get where I am going, I want to be prepared in case a road is blocked and I need to detour or in case I do get lost.

WHAT DO YOU DO IF . . . ? (IT DEPENDS)

Often students starting out as qualitative researchers ask what I call "What do you do if . . ." questions. Some common questions in this genre include:

- What do you do if you cannot get access to the site where you want to collect data?
- What do you do if it seems weird or inappropriate to openly take field notes at the site?
- What do you do if you can't get people at the site to talk to you?
- What do you do if there are too many things to focus on at your site?
- What do you do if you do not think you will be able to answer the research question you want to answer?
- What do you do if your key informant becomes gravely ill?
- What do you do if you hate going to your research site?
- What do you do if you become ill and cannot go to the site?
- What do you do if someone at the site is doing harm to others?
- What do you do if you suspect you may unintentionally be doing harm to others at the site?
- What do you do if you think you are not learning anything new at your research site?

The list of these types of questions could go on for pages. This is because there are an infinite number of "what if" questions that can get asked about any study. There are logistical questions about the study that have to do with resources and time. There are ethical questions about the behavior of the people you are studying as well as your role as a researcher. There are theoretical questions about how you know you are learning anything worth knowing as you conduct your research. My answer to almost all of these questions is always the same: "It depends."[8]

"It depends" is often a frustrating answer to beginning researchers. As travelers in a foreign land, novices often rightly want to know the "rules of the road." Sometimes this answer seems like a cop-out. Surely there are some hard and fast "do's and don'ts" for qualitative researchers? It turns out that there are precious few hard and fast rules of the road—and the first hard and fast "rule" is that the first answer to "What do I do if questions" is "It depends."

"It depends" is not a cute way of trying to wriggle out of answering legitimate questions about how one does qualitative research. (Think Bill Clinton in his impeachment hearing rambling on about how his answer "depended on" the meaning of the word "is.") Rather, it is an answer that first stems from the qualitative epistemological paradigm. There is no one truth but rather a truth that is contextually bound and interpreted. Qualitative research is, by definition, an "it depends" science. We are not searching for generalizability. We are not trying to make claims about how the world in general works. What we are doing is trying to make claims about how a particular slice of the world works and how people in a specific location (spatial, theoretical, and metaphorical) understand their world and specific actions and meanings in it. While ethnographies cannot make claims to be generalizable to a population in the statistical sense, they can and do provide insight into groups of people that can inform our understanding of the larger world around us. Good ethnographers understand that the answers to many of these "What if" questions depend on the context of the research and the question guiding the study. However, there are a few hard-and-fast rules of the road that you can use to guide your ethnographic journey.

CONTEXT, QUESTION, COLLECTING DATA

Context

Okay, so, it depends, but what does it depend on? Travelers to new countries want and need to learn the local customs. Is this a country where they drive on the left side of the road? Is it safe to drink the water? People keep staring at me. Am I doing something wrong? The reason the answer is still "It depends" is that each research site is like its own foreign country. Each organization, place, and people, even if the latter are located in the same geographical vicinity, has its own logic. Thus the answer to "What if . . ." often depends upon the context for the study.

The context of the site matters and will influence the study. Thus, after telling students that the answer to their "What if" question is "It depends," I often ask them about their site, especially if the "What if . . ." question has to do with how to go about the process of collecting data at the site. Where are you observing? What have you learned so far about how this place works? If it feels weird to have a pen and pad out at a particular site, why do you think that is so? If people clam up when you are around, how can you make them feel more at ease? What norms and customs of the site have you learned so far that can inform how to go about collecting data that will help you learn about this place and these people?

If you have not entered the site yet, I often advise that you learn something about it before going. This is much easier now than it used to be, thanks to Web-based information. But even without the Web, it is often possible and a good idea to learn something about a place or people before beginning actual fieldwork. Start with a general plan for going about learning more at the site, while always remaining open to new questions and unexpected findings that may necessitate a shift in data-collection strategy. If time and resources permit, it is ideal to conduct a small pilot study. I recommend a pilot study for students working on a longer project such as a dissertation or thesis. A pilot study is a smaller preliminary version of the study you intend to carry out. This smaller study helps the researcher to prepare for the larger study by helping to clarify the research question and testing out a methodological approach. Conducting a pilot study often results in a more focused main study.

So context matters. It is a critical variable in determining how to go about your study. What else matters? The question.

The Question

So, two qualitative researchers walk into a bar. They sit down beside each other at the bar and both order a beer. They sit and drink the beer, eat some peanuts from the dish on the bar, pay their tab, and leave. They are in the bar for about a half hour. They are both in the same space during the same period of time doing the same thing. One returns to her office and begins a proposal for a study based on her experience entitled "Serving Them Up: A Study of Bartenders in a Local Pub." The other researcher returns to his office and begins to write his proposal, entitled "Claiming a Seat at the Bar: How Bar Patrons Stake a Claim to a Space" or "Why Did Norm Always Sit at the Same Place on *Cheers*?"

As noted earlier, qualitative research is an interpretivist science. Therefore, many answers to "What if . . ." questions can be answered by gaining greater clarity on the research question being posed. This can create challenges for qualitative researchers because we are not always clear on what our question is, especially at the beginning of the study. Suffice it to say for now that qualitative research is a reflexive interpretivist craft that is frequently marked by going back and forth between data and question as they inform one another on the journey. The relationship between your question and data is another factor that impacts your study and the decisions you make as you go about conducting it.

In the example above two researchers observed in the same bar and came away with completely different questions. They likely entered the bar with different interests and concerns. They also almost certainly focused on different aspects of the interaction they observed at the site. Although they were in exactly the same place at the same time, their different research questions likely resulted in vastly different data collection strategies and different decisions about data collection at the site.

Collecting Data

So all of this influences what you actually do at the site, where you sit or stand, how you take field notes, how and when you talk to people, even what you wear to the site. As you begin to think about your own qualitative project, you might find it useful to actually collect some data in order to learn from experience what it might be like.

An Observational Exercise for Practice

In order to try this exercise you will need to set aside about an hour of time. You will need to select a place where you want to observe. Imagine you are a researcher with an interest in food-buying behavior in supermarkets, especially the degree to which people are or are not aware of the nutritional value of their food choices. You have a hunch that most people do not spend too much time selecting the food they buy. They have a list of items they usually buy and they go to the market and quickly select them and check out. You are planning to go to your local supermarket to learn more about how people actually shop and to test out your hunches.

Before you go to observe at your site, the local supermarket, you will want to take a few, say about 5, minutes and think about the research problem: What do you already know about this topic? What about it particularly interests you? What questions about it come to mind? How would you study (observe) it? Write down a list of ideas about: (1) the goals of your research and (2) the kinds of observations that you would need to make in order to explore these goals. If possible and appropriate you might be able to pose a formal research question.

With your list of questions and thoughts on how to observe this phenomenon and a blank notebook in hand, you head to the store. Once you arrive there, there will be a variety of decisions you must make: Which section of the store should I focus? What is going on there that is important, or interesting, that's related to the research question? How do I make these observations? Do I watch people? Interactions? Settings? What level of behavior do I focus on (details of peoples' gestures, for instance, or global summaries of their "style")? Do I concentrate only on a few things, or do I sample from many? Should I count things? Do I take notes, and if so, should these be narratives, outlines, or shorthand accounts? Do I announce myself or remain as unobtrusive as possible? How thorough do I need to be? And so on. You will have many decisions to make. But you must think quickly because you want to limit this exercise to 45 minutes.

While you are in the store, write some field notes. What did people say and do? Try to capture actual conversations. Try to get thick rich detail about what you are noticing. What do people look like? What do they say? What do they do? What seem to be their motivations? Did you identify yourself? If so, how? What do you think was the effect of your presence in the field setting? Were there things that you were not able to observe? And most important, What did you learn relevant to your research question(s)?

During this 45-minute period try also to interview at least one person in this setting. In doing this you will have a number of decisions to make. Who will you interview? What will you ask them? Will you take notes? What will you tell them about your study? After the interview write up your field notes, including a brief description of your informant(s). Why did you choose this person to interview? What was said in the interview? What did you learn from the interview related to your research question?

After 45 minutes you leave the site and go to a quiet spot or return home to "process" your experience. Take a few minutes to look over your field notes and interview notes. What did you learn about the fieldwork process? What would you do differently? What worked well? Why? What did not work well? Why? Finally, notice all of the decisions that you made in the field. Why did you make them? Would you make them again next time?

Implicit in this exercise is the understanding that the decisions the researcher makes in the field are connected both to context and question. Whom you choose to talk with will depend on both who you happen upon at the site (context) and who you seek out based on your interest (question). What you decide to ask people is driven both by what you want to learn (question) and who you happen to interview (context). So qualitative research is a contingent science—a variation on "it depends." It depends on your site, on your question, and on why and how you want to collect data. Are there no absolute rules of the road? Well, yes—now that you ask, there are a few. Below I provide some guidelines to keep in mind as you move on from this trial exercise to your real project.

RULES FOR THE ROAD: NEVER SPIT ON YOUR SHOES

Never Spit on Your Shoes (Cazet, 1990) is the catchy and compelling title of a children's book about a child's first day in 1st grade. Despite the fact that the teacher and class explicitly develop a list of rules for the classroom that includes items such as "raise your hand before calling out" as well as more humorous rules, such as "never spit on your shoes," Arnie is exhausted by learning the rules of his new 1st-grade world. A "traveler" in the "foreign land" of 1st grade, Arnie spends a good bit of his 1st day just trying to understand this strange and new country in which he finds himself. Should he raise his hand to answer questions? Who is the principal and what does she do? Why are the other kids laughing at him? By the end of the day he has arrived home to his mother and a plate of warm cookies with one (humorous) absolute rule generated when the class made rules for their room about surviving life in 1st grade: Never spit on your shoes. For Arnie, starting out in 1st grade is exhausting and bewildering, there are few absolutes, and he is exhausted by trying to learn the language and customs of his new world. Yet despite the confusion created by his new surroundings, he did learn that he should never spit on his shoes.

Similarly, there are precious few absolutes for qualitative travelers. Starting out at a new site is exhausting and bewildering. Learning the language and customs of the people you are studying will take time and energy. However, there are a few absolute rules of the road you can take to the bank as you start out.

Do Not Share Your Field Notes

Guard your field notes with your life. Never show anyone at the site your field notes and never, ever leave your field notes out where someone could inadvertently see them. Why? You should not leave your field notes out for the same reason you do not leave a personal diary lying around. In a diary or in your field notes you are thinking and writing freely in an effort to make sense of the world around you. The thoughts are uncensored and can be hurtful to others. Having a participant in your study see your field notes could undermine your entire study.[9]

Be Careful What You Promise

Similarly, I caution students to be very circumspect in promising anything to their participants in return for joining in the study. At times researchers will pay study participants a small amount. However, often people participate in research without payment. It is often tempting to promise to show the people at your site the report or dissertation you will write. As others have noted, this can be very painful (Lareau, 2011; Whyte, 1943/1993). While there are compelling reasons to share your work with the study participants (e.g., a desire for research to inform practice, the desire to "give back" something to people who have generously shared so much with you), it is generally not recommended that you do this before the end of your study. While it may be reasonable to have participants check interview transcripts for accuracy, sharing preliminary findings with them is unwise.

Be Curious

Qualitative research is fraught. It requires emotional and social skills. It winds its way into your personal life and takes a great deal of time and energy. Given these drawbacks, it is important that the researcher have a genuine curiosity about the world and the particular social world or process she wants to study. It will propel and sustain you on your journey.

A genuine intense curiosity about a particular place and population will also likely endear you to the people you are studying. We all like to have someone pay attention to us and what we do. It is fun to explain how and why we do what we do. Your curiosity about the topic or population will usually be welcomed by the people you are studying.

A strong sense of curiosity is also a hedge of sorts against agenda-driven research. Rather than being motivated by wanting to prove something, it is better to be curious about something. For instance, instead of entering the field trying to show that teacher expectations affect student learning, a strong sense of curiosity about what affects student outcomes or what effect teacher expectations have on students is a much better approach. The purpose of the research is to explore a topic or question rather than to prove a hunch. While it is important to be aware of and perhaps even explore hunches or hypotheses, this method of inquiry is not meant to test them.

GAINING ACCESS TO A SITE: GETTING IN AND GAINING INSTITUTIONAL REVIEW BOARD (IRB) APPROVAL

When I first started doing qualitative research in graduate school, I was most concerned with gaining access to my site. Would the schools where I wanted to collect data let me observe? Would people I wanted to talk to allow me to interview them? These are reasonable and widely shared concerns. It is, in fact, a bit scary to ask for the kind of access you think you will need to carry out a study. I think it is frightening for me because I know, much more so than the participant, what really I am asking for.

When I ask someone to participate in a study, what I am really asking for is a favor, and not an insignificant one at that. I am asking for people to allow me to hang around and watch them in their place of work or recreation or home. I know I will, in fact, intrude on their lives and I will take their time by asking questions and politely badgering them for materials that might be useful (handouts, reports, other documents) and take even more of their time when I interview them. And though most research participants do not realize it no matter how often and emphatically it is explained to them, the process will be intrusive in some ways. Through the process they may learn things about themselves, their colleagues, or their organization that may be unpleasant or that may surprise them. They may also learn some pleasant things. They may enjoy, as I have found many participants do, the opportunity to talk with someone who is really interested in their work or their children or why they believe the world works as it does. Either way, they will not be left untouched by the process.

Knowing the degree to which participants are likely to be touched by their participation, I take the process of gaining entry to a site very seriously. In addition to "getting in," I am interested in making sure that to the greatest extent possible the participants in my studies have a sense of what to expect from their participation. I try to be as explicit as possible as I describe what the study will be about. In addition to having key participants and those who will be interviewed for the project read and sign Informed Consent documents (issues of informed consent and IRB will be taken up shortly), I also spend time talking with them about the study and answering questions about their participation. The first step, however, is making initial contact with someone at the place you want to study and requesting their approval.

Getting In

It is usually best to ask someone if you can observe in their school, library, store, and so on in person. Sometimes this can be hard. As you start out and are trying to gain access to a site for fieldwork you may be unsure of what you want to study. You may not even be sure that this place is the right place to start. But you have to start somewhere and that means you have to gain access to a site for fieldwork. Go about this aspect of your project with substantial care and attention. The success of your first contact can be the difference between getting in and being turned down and having to find another site. Think about what you might say. Write it out and practice what you might say and then determine who the right person is to ask and how to ask that person face-to-face. Consult more experienced student colleagues, professional colleagues, and your professors. Find the right words to describe in sufficient (but not too much) detail what it is you want to do. Be polite, direct, honest, and brief. Offer to follow up with more information. It is hard to turn down a reasonable request made from a friendly, unassuming, polite person standing in front of you. It is really easy to delete an e-mail.

Sometimes it is almost impossible to ask in person. Some of the people from whom you will need to be granted access have secretaries who screen calls and sit outside offices. Resist the temptation to lie in wait and surprise the person you want to ask. This is usually not an effective strategy. Many people resent surprise asking. A better strategy is to make friends with the secretary or gatekeeper. Explain to them, in a brief, direct, and honest way, what it is you want to do and ask them how best to gain approval. Sometimes this works, sometimes it does not.

For instance, you might say, "I know Superintendent Smith is a very busy person. Perhaps I can explain to you what I am trying to do? I am a graduate student at State University. I want to study mid-career teachers. I am interested in why they stay in teaching. I would like to observe and interview four mid-career teachers at Elmwood Elementary. The principal at Elmwood Elementary is a friend from grad school and is interested in the study but she needs formal written approval from the Superintendent to allow me into the school. What do you think is the best way to make this request of Superintendent Smith? I know he has a lot on his plate."

Notice the brevity and direct nature of this request. I did not cite research on the need to retain teachers or talk about how great Elmwood Elementary is. I said what I wanted to do and what I needed from Dr. Smith. I also tried to express an understanding of the reality of Dr. Smith's job.

If you cannot get in front of the person who can grant you access, the next best method is the telephone. Try finding out when the person will be available. Let the gatekeeper know you will only need 3 to 5 minutes of her time—and stick to it. As a last resort, there are times when a carefully worded (yes, again), brief, direct, and honest e-mail or letter is the only way to ask for access. In this letter or verbally over the phone or in person your goal is to describe what it is you want to *do*. You do not need to explain the theoretical underpinnings of your study. Most people are not interested. What they are interested in is how your presence in the school, library, or coffee shop will affect them and the other people there.

This issue of gaining entry and access is not a one-time event. Access is usually negotiated over the course of a project. While a researcher may need permission of one leader in an organization in order to "officially" collect data there, the process of educating the many individuals you will observe or interview over the course of a months-long project is ongoing and access is negotiated at many different levels within the organization or site.

Usually when I collect data at a school, I gain initial access at the site through an informal contact. Perhaps I know a teacher or administrator at the school or know someone who knows someone at the school. Sometimes I do not know anyone at a given school and simply approach the principal. Usually, no matter how the first contact is initiated—through informal networks or a "cold call"—the principal must support the project. Once I have gained support of the principal, I then proceed with the other steps of gaining entry, such as being approved by the school district and my university Institutional Review Board, a process I explain below. Once I have official approval at the site I am usually introduced by the principal at a faculty meeting and/or a parent at a Home and School (Parent Teacher Association/ Parent Teacher Organization) meeting. Even once I have gained official entry to the site and have been formally introduced to the community I expect to constantly be explaining what I am doing at the site and gaining access from individuals there.

Most organizations (schools, businesses, nonprofit organizations) are complex places, with several employees and many constituencies. Not all of them may have been at the meeting or meetings where you were introduced. And if they were at the meeting they may not have been paying attention or may not have really understood from the brief introduction provided who you are and why you are hanging around. Therefore, you need to assume very low levels of understanding about you and your project throughout the organization. You must understand that even though you have gained access to a school, for example, you still need to gain access to individual classrooms, meetings, or other social spaces within the organization. As I detail in Chapter 3, a brief, honest, and straightforward explanation usually suffices. If, however, this person may be a key participant at the site, you might want to offer a longer explanation. If you are seeking access to their office or desire to interview them you will want to provide more detailed information regarding the study and their potential involvement in it. You will also need to get their informed consent.

Informed Consent and IRB

One of the more fear-inducing topics for students conducting research for the first time is often the dreaded Institutional Review Board (IRB). They exist at every university where research is conducted, and are in place to review the data collection procedures of every study conducted at the university that engages with live human beings to ensure that reasonable precautions have been taken to protect the people participating in the research. This research must be approved whether or not it will be published. If you are doing research with real live people, even if it seems innocuous to you—such as asking what kind of coffee they like and why—you need IRB approval.[10] Your IRB will have a set of procedures for you to follow to gain approval and they will require you to get the informed consent of your research participants. Usually this informed consent is a form that is signed by the participant. There are very good reasons for this protection. Horrible things have been done to people in the name of science.[11] So while the level of scrutiny given a researcher interested in a relatively low-risk study such as an investigation of teacher attitudes about technology use in their classrooms may seem overly much, there are good reasons for these protections.

I think that students (and professors, for that matter) find these review boards so daunting for a few reasons. First, they are daunting because they can stop a project in its tracks. Without approval from the review board, the project cannot continue. They can also be daunting because of the length of time the process can take. I believe they are also daunting because the review process usually requires a detailed explanation of what you plan to do, why you want to do it, how it will benefit society and how you will protect the rights of your study participants. Thus, the review boards are asking questions that many qualitative researchers find difficult to answer during the initial stages of a project. Because qualitative research often unfolds over the course of a study as the research question becomes clearer through fieldwork, it is often hard to state at the outset what, exactly, you plan to do. Despite this limitation, my advice is to request approval for your study as soon as possible and do the best you can to describe what you want to do and why.

In writing initial applications to the Review Board I often imagine what I would like to have happen as the project unfolds. For instance, I cannot usually say exactly how many people I will interview, but I can estimate. I may not have a complete interview protocol drafted and it may change slightly over time, but I try to produce a good-faith version of what it will be like in the final form. I write about what I think I will do, knowing that the interview questions may change slightly, that I may interview more or fewer people than I propose, and that the focus of my study may shift slightly over time. If the study is approved and during data collection I find that the focus changes in a substantive way or I need to interview people who had not been approved by the initial proposal (e.g., the initial proposal included parents but not school administrators), I submit a request for an amendment.

The standards and implementation practices of Institutional Review Boards vary from one institution to another, so it is important to be familiar with the ins and outs of yours. The paperwork required varies from one institution to another, as does the schedule on which submissions are considered. I generally do not recommend seeking approval for a study in the very early stages when the researcher may be talking with people at the site about participation. I also do not request approval from the IRB if I am observing in a public place for a brief (two to three observations) amount of time, such as in a supermarket or coffee shop or on the street. If I am planning to conduct formal or informal interviews I then seek IRB approval. If you have questions about when and how to seek approval it is always better to ask your own IRB office. They are more than likely happy to help and will tell you what you need to know. Institutional Review Boards often have specific language that they want in consent forms and their own procedures and process for review. The worst mistake you can make when you are conducting research on your own that is not under the auspices of a class such as dissertation or thesis research is to collect data for a study that should have been reviewed by the IRB without seeking approval. This puts your study as well as your university in jeopardy. It is your responsibility as a researcher to be aware of the standards at your institution and to work diligently to meet them.

Sometimes there can be a bit of a "chicken-and-egg" problem with review boards. There have been times when a school district has required approval from the IRB before they would issue an approval of the study but the IRB would not issue approval until they had a letter from the school district stating their approval. While this is frustrating, I have been able to communicate the problem to both the district and the IRB and reach a satisfactory resolution. (In my case the IRB issued a conditional approval pending a letter from the district. Then the district wrote a letter of support.) Administrative details can be maddening and may seem overly bureaucratic. Be patient and remember that everyone is trying their best to protect the people in your study. If you plan on working with a particularly vulnerable population that is treated with special protection under human subject guidelines as a "protected" population, such as children, pregnant women, or prisoners, your approval process will likely be more rigorous and time-consuming and you should plan accordingly.

BEGINNING

Beginning an ethnographic project is exciting and frightening at the same time. It is a time full of possibility. The researcher is like a painter with an open canvas, free to select any vista to paint in any style they choose. There are so many decisions to make and for a beginner the landscape may seem to be full of land mines—mistakes waiting to be made.

There is, however, only one way to begin, and that is to start. Take a deep breath. Enjoy the sense of excitement and expectation that most new experiences bring. Take delight in the energy of a new project. Remember that there is no such thing as a perfect study and that you will make mistakes. Prepare as best you can for your project and learn from your mistakes.

NOTES

1. There are examples of qualitative work that have had broad significance, usually by changing our way of thinking about a process. Annette Lareau's book *Unequal Childhoods* (2011) changed the way that many think about childrearing in the United States. As I note later in the book, Jean Claude Piaget and Elisabeth Kubler-Ross studied specific processes in depth over many years and influenced how we think about childhood (Piaget) and death (Kubler-Ross). These kinds of field-changing qualitative studies are, however, rare and data collection often spans several years.

2. All subjects' names, throughout the book, are pseudonyms.

3. A paper based on this study can be found in Cucchiara & Horvat, 2009.

4. The full study can be found in Horvat & Davis, 2011.

5. The classic example illustrating the difficulty of making causal claims comes from the research linking lung cancer to smoking. For many years researchers were able to establish that there was a correlation between smoking and lung cancer by documenting that people who smoked had higher rates of cancer. However, they were unable to link smoking and cancer in a causal way. To "show" or "prove" this claim, a randomized controlled study would have to be conducted. It was not until the 1950s, when large-scale statistical studies were conducted, that smoking was definitively shown to cause increased rates of lung cancer.

6. While Piaget's work has been challenged by other prominent psychologists, most notably Lev Vygotsky, many of his ideas are still central concepts in child development.

7. While at times using a laptop can be appropriate for data collection and it can speed up the process of writing field notes, one distinct disadvantage can be the need to ensure its safety while you are at the site. In addition, if you have a laptop with you, you may be far less mobile and need to be prepared to bring it with you wherever you go. The same can be said about newer tablet computers and other devices, though they are more easily portable. They can be quite useful for fieldwork, but you need to be congnizant of the degree to which they are appropriate for the research context and address how to keep them safe and secure while doing fieldwork.

8. As a student I was both infuriated and perplexed by Harold Levine's seemingly constant use of the term "it depends." While the phrase is widely used in a variety of contexts, the way I use it here draws on Harold's use of the phrase as a way to teach students the often contingent nature of qualitative research.

9. There are some times when researchers very deliberately choose to share data, such as interview transcripts or emergent analysis, with participants at the site. These types of techniques will be taken up in Chapter 5. The important point here is that these efforts to share data with participants are deliberate. They are planned in advance and they generally do not occur during the early phases of a study.

10. The only exception to this at my institution is that if you are doing research as a part of a class you do not need individual IRB approval. Because the research is being conducted as a part of a course, it is the professor's responsibility to ensure that the correct protections are in place for human subjects. This may vary from institution to institution.

11. For instance, the infamous Tuskegee Syphilis Study, conducted from 1932–1972, studied the progression of syphilis among poor rural black men. These men were not informed of the true purpose of the study and were not treated for syphilis even after a safe and effective treatment—penicillin—had become available and widely used elsewhere. The abuses in this study led to reform in the treatment of research participants. For more information please see http://www.cdc.gov/tuskegee/index.html

ERIN HORVAT

In this chapter, Mary Lou Heron, a 3rd-year doctoral student, recounts her qualitative journey. In her narration she addresses some of the most common problems that students encounter. She also recounts her initial lack of understanding about and skepticism toward qualitative research. In the narrative she describes how, through conducting a small study, she came to understand the value of the approach. Mary Lou's reflections on her journey ultimately are most valuable to the novice as she explores how she managed to find and make meaning in completing her first ethnographic project—which involved many changes, reformulations, and recalculations over the course of the project.

Like many beginners, Mary Lou worked hard to do "everything right." A seasoned professional by the end of the required coursework for her doctorate, she was focused on successfully completing my Qualitative Data course and moving on to her dissertation. She was not looking for adventure. However, as is often the case, adventure found Mary Lou. Through the twists and turns of her qualitative journey, she provides real-life examples of many of the concepts and suggestions from Chapter 1, including the importance of patience and a willingness to tolerate ambiguity. She also introduces some data collection and analysis techniques I cover in more depth in Chapter 3. Finally, this chapter addresses some of the more practical concerns related to locating and gaining entry into a feasible site and beginning fieldwork.

In this reflection on her qualitative journey Mary Lou also provides significant insights into how she moved back and forth between emerging patterns at her site, relevant literature, and her interest in literacy practices as she searched for the story of her site. While she entered her site with a firm desire to focus on literacy practices, she found herself motivated by understanding other compelling questions related to the literacy activities that were occurring at her site. In the end, with a good deal of persistence and effort, she was able to learn how to do qualitative research and answer an interesting research question.

From the First Site to the Third Place

Finding Meaning and a Research Site That Works

Mary Lou Heron

I was a reluctant and skeptical student of qualitative research. Prior to en-rolling in Dr. Horvat's class, my understanding of qualitative research came from an abundance of book reading, with little practical experience. This incomplete and somewhat inaccurate knowledge of qualitative methods led me to have certain beliefs about the method and led me to be skeptical about pursuing a qualitative line of inquiry. I believed that qualitative studies took a long time, required the researcher to reflect on issues from different angles, and generated words and descriptions rather than numerical data. Finally, I was not so sure of the worthiness of the conclusions that might be drawn from qualitative investigations. Was there a case for conducting research if an outcome was not definitive? For a student who wanted to complete her doctoral program as expeditiously as possible and grew weary even think-ing about reflexivity, qualitative inquiry did not appear to be a good match. I was interested in making claims such as, "in 9 out of 10 cases, research shows that . . ." or "75% of the time, respondents believed that . . ." State-ments such as these, surely, were the haute cuisine of investigatory methods. Given the choice and based on my preconceived notions, I was convinced that a quantitative rather than a qualitative study was *the* way to conduct research. I was also reasonably confident that the exploration for my dis-sertation would align itself more closely to quantitative measures, although my final topic had yet to be clearly outlined. Nonetheless, the qualitative research methods course was a required component of my graduate studies. I soon discovered how much there was to learn.

In the narrative that follows I share my exploration into qualitative in-quiry. While most journeys have twists and turns along the road, my quali-tative travels were unusually circuitous. This slower and more challenging route to learning qualitative research methods taught me a great deal about the importance of choosing a good site for conducting qualitative inquiry and about how to find meaning in the actions and words of the people I studied. In what follows I share these lessons I learned about how to locate and select a good site for a qualitative project and how to find something worth writing about at the site. I also provide real-life examples about the importance of packing a tolerance for ambiguity and a sense of adventure with you on your journey.

One of the first assignments in Dr. Horvat's class was to reflect upon and complete a Site Selection Prospectus (included in the Appendix). The guidelines, which I read several times, proved to be my anchor in my long and winding journey. The probing questions—Who will you be observing? What will you observe? Where will your observations take place? Why will you be observing at this site?—provided a framework for my inquiry and also serve as the foundation for this chapter. Through finding the answers to these who, what, where, and why questions, I was ultimately able to find and answer an interesting research question at my site. Along the way I also learned to appreciate the value of uncovering meaning in studying participants' words, actions, and thoughts.

BEGINNING THE JOURNEY

Prior to the start of the semester, Dr. Horvat e-mailed course participants to alert us to begin the search for a research site. I began to consider options even though many questions were left unanswered. What kind of site would lend itself to the demands of the course? What might I be doing in the selected site? Are all sites created equal? Are there characteristics that define the perfect site? In truth, my focus was on completing another set of course requirements as efficiently as I could. How important was the actual site? Finally, I was determined that meeting the requirements for this research course would be framed to include my interest in investigating literacy practices. As I neared the end of graduate coursework, it was time to bring my dissertation topic into clearer focus. I hoped that the completion of each assignment in the qualitative research course would bring me one step closer to my goal.

I first considered a location close to home, knowing that I would be spending a great deal of time observing there. The remaining criteria specified in course objectives were rather vague but I was confident that after jumping in, clarity would come. I began to cross things off the list of site requirements. A physical space, well-defined—check. Space where there was continuity to activities—check. Site where one could gain access—check.

Other considerations included specifying who and what one might observe at the site and why the potential site might be viable for conducting research. The parameters seemed to fit any number of potential locations, with the target being so broad that I thought hitting the bull's-eye would be relatively straightforward. I selected the library at a local, very small private college (total enrollment of 1,000 students, including undergraduate, graduate, and seminary), expecting that a library would be the perfect venue for investigating literacy practices. This was Plan A and I was ready to begin my search for meaning within a context—an idea that I would be learning a great deal about. We were encouraged to visit the site very early in the semester to begin documenting happenings there. My first visits were dedicated to noting both physical details of the library and the types of activities that occurred during my visits. Jackson Hall, a three-story building where the library was located, was erected in 1919. The structure was well maintained, with highly polished stonework, imposing oak doors, and stained-glass windows. I wasn't sure which activities or routines would later become grist for the mill in my investigation, so I was careful to record what I felt were even insignificant details—such as two students at a library table huddled together over a text, a lone coed briefly visiting the curriculum materials area, and a lone student perched on a library stool in front of a computer.

Early on in the qualitative research course, class time was devoted to sharing goings-on at each of the class members' research sites. We were grouped into small groups of "critical friends" to provide strategic feedback and support as we, as a class, stumbled forward to meet course objectives. At an initial sharing, each class member was encouraged to describe his or her research site along with initial impressions of the types of activities that would be observed during the semester. One of the early course goals was to begin to think analytically about the selected site in order to develop a research question related to goings-on at the site (see Chapter 6, by Bradley Bergey, on developing questions). After the first several hours of observing at the college library, I was somewhat disheartened by the lack of activity and frankly shared my frustrations with my critical friends group in the course. I had spent over 3½ hours and documented very little beyond a physical description of a very stately venue. Of note were empty study carrels, blank computer screens, vacant library tables, and books abandoned on tables. During my first visit, a total of 16 patrons used the library's resources, some staying for mere minutes. The quiet of the library, broken only by the hum of fluorescent lighting, was deafening. It was impossible to manufacture either library patrons or the hustle and bustle that generally accompanies college campus libraries. With the first set of field notes completed, I began to feel somewhat skeptical that the library would yield any significant data to analyze. How, in fact, might one report on and subsequently analyze nothing of note? My critical friends dutifully listened to my tale of woe. Several in the group asked thoughtful, probing questions in an effort to unearth something that perhaps I'd missed during the first several visits and hours at the library. A couple of suggestions emerged—try a different time of day; try a day other than the weekend; and above all, a hearty, "Don't abandon the site!"

With a welcomed bit of encouragement and armed with new resolve, I ventured back to the college library, visiting at different hours and days, hopeful that things might change. I determined to forge ahead and not abandon the site for at least one more set of observational data. I recorded all of my thoughts and wonderings for the next set of required field notes. My optimism, however, was short-lived. There continued to be a paucity of patrons as well as activity at the library. An additional 6 hours and just 13 library users were generating little of interest. Most patrons came and went within minutes, checking out or returning materials. I was still not sure if I was on point with what qualitative researchers are expected to accomplish during site visits and was becoming increasingly disenchanted with the library as a research site. During the next opportunity to share site updates, I tried, in as much detail as I could muster, to describe the "nothing" and the prolonged lack of library activity. As I attempted to paint a picture of the limited goings-on in the college library, I had hoped to convince my critical friends that it was, indeed, time to abandon the site and begin looking for a more opportune venue. Indeed, several of my critical friends found it difficult to believe that so little could occur in a college library. Describing nothing had been a challenge, but I, too, had misgivings about leaving my first site behind. The lack of activity as well as the lack of actual library patrons would make it just about impossible to search for meaning . . . there was little to search through.

I needed to adjust my game plan. Why had the library become a dead end? Everything seemed to be in place to promote use—computers, copiers, quiet study areas, resources for projects, hours of operation, helpful librarians—yet glaringly absent were people taking advantage of the available resources. What were my other options? I was making negligible progress toward developing skills as a qualitative researcher. Somewhat discouraged yet not disheartened, I sought counsel from Dr. Horvat, explained my frustrations, and ultimately began planning an exodus from the library. Once again I poured over criteria for selecting a viable research site. What had I missed the first time around? And more important, how could I avoid making the same mistakes again? After all, the time line for completing course requirements called for assignment submissions in a timely manner. Step one was finding a viable site where I could begin to collect data—grist for the qualitative research mill, as it were. Nothing to document meant nothing to mull over and analyze. I needed something to talk about and visits to the library weren't providing that something.

A PAUSE

I offer a bit of reflection before moving on. What was lost or gained as a result of the time and energy already expended? A loss—clearly, I had been frustrated. How could a potential research site yield so little? Could the experience have been avoided? The library met the suggested criteria as a reasonable choice to conduct qualitative research. It was accessible and open when I could schedule visits; it was a well-defined physical space; and I anticipated that a library would align well with my interest in exploring literacy practices. Was it something that I had done or not done that could have engendered a different outcome?

Trying not to be disheartened, I struggled to look for something I gained from my initial experience as a researcher. At first, I was reasonably confident that there would be more than enough to observe and document at a college library, even a very small one. I learned to look carefully for data that might tell a story. Unfortunately, my first venture into qualitative research generated a very short story with what some might call an unhappy ending. However, I realized upon reflection that I did, unwittingly, learn a couple of critical lessons in this aborted first attempt.

In Chapter 1 Dr. Horvat mentions a couple of things to bring along when starting a qualitative journey. She suggests "packing" a tolerance for ambiguity. For me this meant I had to make peace with the process of finding a site, abandoning it, and then finding a new site. Clearly, I was not sure where I was going or where I'd end up as a result of my visits to the library. I had not expected a "dead end" but resolved to accept it and then, most importantly, charged ahead. I focused on locating a new research site and carefully reviewed site selection criteria. Might conversations logged during class with critical friends help me find perhaps not the *perfect* but rather a *better* site where I would spend time? I was faced with developing Plan B.

So I needed to revisit the qualities that make a site viable and rich with something to observe and subsequently interpret. Why would a particular site be of interest? The guidelines in the course syllabus for site selection were familiar but I returned and read them no longer as a neophyte—after all, I had already invested several hours over several site visits in order to attempt to navigate the qualitative research scene. The questions were targeting the where, who, what, and why of the site. Where would I observe? Who would I be observing? What would I observe? Why observe at the chosen

site? I clearly understood that the intent of the questions was to help focus those who were new to qualitative research. Yet some of the questions,
which on the surface seemed straightforward, became less than clear-cut.
Willis (2007) describes qualitative investigations as "recursive and fuzzy"
(p. 202). For me "recursive" meant revisiting my experiences from different
vantage points in an attempt to extract meaningful ideas. My appreciation
for "fuzzy" was growing as I struggled with finding answers to the questions
of where, who, what, and why. I knew that at some point I would, indeed,
reach the end of the course with my challenges resolved and with some sort
of finished product.

WAS THIS A WORTHY PLAN B?

As I moved toward Plan B, I considered any site that was related to my area
of interest, literacy practices. My quest ultimately landed me at a nearby
bookstore chain. It was accessible and I anticipated that there were likely
plenty of literacy-related activities. I could explore which book titles were
currently popular or whether one age group was more heavily represented
than another or even if the availability of electronic reading materials could
eliminate the need for bookstores in the future. In multiple drive-bys, I had
noted that the parking lot was often bustling, regardless of the weather
or particular gift-giving season. The bookstore appeared to be a popular
destination for many and it appeared large enough to garner a fair amount
of traffic, hopefully more than the college library. Accessible, well-defined
physical space, interesting—it met all three criteria!

The store itself was rather large, with networks of bookshelves set up
in clusters running perpendicular as well as parallel to one another, marking
off areas of potential interest—sections for children's books, media, best-
selling books, young adult books, cookbooks. During one of my early trips
to the bookstore, I realized that I would need to narrow my focus. There
appeared to be too many areas to manage for this project. Should I station
myself by the children's books? Or hang out by the CDs? Perhaps camp out
by the best-sellers? Each would likely yield different data with a potentially
different demographic. I wondered how it would be possible to manage collecting data in any or all of these areas, and the thought of navigating the
entire store seemed overwhelming. I needed to refine my game plan.

There was another area, which was unmistakably noticeable when entering the store because of the distinctive aroma emanating from the front
corner of the building—namely, the bookstore café, a homey spot with
plenty of seating where folks could casually and comfortably peruse reading material. I decided to investigate its "site-worthiness" (did it meet the

criteria for a viable research site?) as my "well-defined physical space" to begin to gather data. Tables and chairs were positioned to promote conversation or to allow solitary activity. There was a seating area, complete with leather club chairs, across the front of the store that had intentionally been arranged to feel like a cozy living room. The coffee shop offered multiple vantage points that might work for me to watch goings-on there. It was a place where I could dissolve into the landscape as an unobtrusive observer, at least for the early part of my journey. Since I was still learning about qualities that would confirm a site as *good* or *better*, it did occur to me that this site, too, might prove to be unproductive. I was looking for the right venue for my project and was thinking about all the recommended criteria, systematically checking off each one. It was definitely accessible and interesting and, as far as I could tell, there was more than a fair amount of action with people both reading and interacting with one another around books. For the time being, I decided that this site might work. Committed to the bookstore café and keeping fingers crossed that I could experience some success at doing qualitative work, I believed I was moving in the right direction. This would be my *where*.

Feeling relatively confident with my new location, I was ready to jump into addressing next questions. But where to start? In Chapter 3, Dr. Horvat uses a vacuuming metaphor. The metaphor provides useful guidance for novice researchers like me who don't quite know what might be noteworthy. What might eventually become important to address a research question? Her advice is, suck up everything! I started to vacuum. I noted sights, sounds, and smells. The café was frequently crowded with an accompanying hum of conversation. Distinctive coffee and chocolate aromas seemed to draw folks to the café. I began to watch people and make notes on activities that occurred consistently. There was plenty to document. And in the back of my mind, I wondered how the activity would point me to a worthy question.

People came to peruse magazines. Current issues on a variety of topics—sports, health, knitting, gardening—were arranged on racks next to the café. There were no restrictions on browsing, so stacks of magazines were frequently left on tables to be enjoyed by all, and often became topics of conversation when table guests changed. It was the same for books—again, easily accessible with lots of options. Several café patrons sampled best sellers or skimmed through stacks of books on chosen topics prior to purchasing. Baristas periodically strolled through the café, often engaging customers in casual conversation, as they scooped up unwanted items to return to shelves. Most patrons purchased drinks and snacks in the café but it was unclear whether the food items were the primary enticement for the people who gathered there. I sensed that something else might be at work.

So I had found my *where*. There was plenty of action in the café. But despite all of the possible literacy activities I could examine at the café, I had yet to formulate a good question that would allow my investigation to have a clear direction. I was ready to consider my next question, the *who*. Although seemingly straightforward, I was faced with a couple of choices. In contrast to the small college library, the bookstore café provided plenty of "someones" to watch. Who would inform my investigation at the café— baristas, café patrons, bookstore clerks? Rather quickly, I eliminated both the baristas and the bookstore clerks. There were only a couple of baristas on duty at a time and clerks were more apt to spend time helping customers on the main floor of the bookstore. So of the groups that emerged, the patrons seemed to be the logical choice. Since there were more café patrons than either baristas or clerks, I predicted that there would be more interactions to document. Because the patrons weren't limited by work demands like the baristas and clerks were, I hoped the interactions would be more diverse and potentially more interesting. And access to the café patrons would be simple. I could sit just about anywhere in the café to note actions and interactions. I could become part of the crowd by purchasing a beverage and, as my cover, glance through a current periodical or best seller. Either would preserve my anonymity while allowing me to watch all activity in the café. I could document patrons' activities or conversations without drawing attention to myself.

Two questions remained. *Why* would the café make a good research site? *What*, exactly, was I going to be watching or watching for? As I focused on the who, what, where, and why, my research project would likely take shape. Clearly the café provided opportunities to investigate a complete array of literacy practices—reading, writing, listening, speaking. However, reading, listening, and speaking were most heavily represented during my visits and offered many of the interactions that I would document. Although I observed a few instances of writing, they tended to be solitary activities, with infrequent contact between café patrons.

So what would be my focus? Should I consider the types of activities in which patrons were engaged? More reading? Listening? Speaking? What about demographic information? More retired people or couples? More of one generation than another? Was gender a consideration? Would types of reading material that patrons selected be research-worthy? Perhaps I could compare the number of literacy activities to other pastimes I observed. Did more people come to read than for other purposes? What were other potential reasons that people came to the bookstore café and were they at all related to literacy? All possible considerations. The questions swirled and along the way, I looked for patterns in patron behavior. At this point in data collection, I had not considered a grounded theory lens, but retrospectively it made sense. It would take thoughtfully digging into and organizing the data to explain what I saw going on at the café. Ultimately the data would lead me to a hypothesis that would help me to explain café activity. For now, however, I continued to ponder different areas of potential focus, collect data, use the opportunities for reflection afforded by the memo-writing requirements for class, and reflect on my data as I tried to focus on an answerable question. I also found myself growing slightly more comfortable with the ambiguity of the whole qualitative research enterprise.

Now that I had a where and who, I was ready to consider the what. There was more than enough activity in the café. I counted no fewer than ten patrons during any of my visits, and on more than one occasion there was standing room only. I saw many patrons enter the building and gravitate directly toward the café. Some I labeled as "café regulars." They were predictably present when I was at the site collecting data. In early field notes they were described physically, but later on as I got to know several of them, I was able to refer to them by name. They often engaged in the same tasks—browsing reading material, meeting friends, studying, using Wi-Fi. They often sat in the same locations—the comfy leather chairs, a six-top table in the middle of the café, a table on the perimeter. I deduced that the café was clearly a destination for a fair number of the people who turned up there. There was something more here to consider. But what was it?

SEARCHING FOR MEANING

Qualitative researchers are on a quest to understand the meaning of things within a context. Would data I was collecting cluster in recognizable patterns to help me explain why people visited the bookstore café, or shed light on their literacy practices? The first few visits to the bookstore café yielded what turned out to be fascinating observational data. Although, as yet, I was not sure what I might be looking for or at, I began to see patterns almost immediately. I was uncertain, however, if the patterns would become significant or meaningful during my eventual interpretation and analysis of the data. My visits often occurred during the early evening or on weekends. I devoted chunks of time to observing activities and was not surprised by the typical café happenings—beverage purchases, Wi-Fi access, magazine and book browsing, comfortable conversations among friends—predictable, to be sure. Interestingly, however, there were more than a few café patrons who routinely appeared during many of my visits. At first I thought it might be related to the time of day or day of the week I was there. I later discovered that a café network of sorts was alive and well. There was a unique cast of characters and each appeared, as if on cue, often arriving or engaging, predictably, with other café goers. These were characters I would eventually have the opportunity to meet and build relationships with.

By this point in my journey, I was just a bit behind my classmates. My field notes seemed to blossom. I went from having precious little to document from library visits to having what seemed like volumes in recording café interactions. However, my ability to settle on a meaningful question had been hampered by changing sites. In spite of this setback, I was, in Willis's (2007) words, seeking to "develop emerging insights, hunches, and tentative hypotheses" (p. 202) as I moved forward. Attempting to find meaning in events within a social setting was my ultimate goal and there was definitely more to discuss and comment on in my weekly field notes and memoing assignments as I described my newly embraced research site and its characters. As I approached the midpoint in data collection, I was hoping to make sense out of my data. There seemed to be something about the café that drew patrons. Several intentionally frequented the café. I wondered how to explore this idea more fully.

EMERGING MEANING

I had already sensed that there might be at least a couple of reasons why the café was so attractive to people. Perhaps for some, visiting the café was part of a predictable routine. It was a place where beverage and pastry selections were abundant. Perhaps the company or opportunities for conversation drew others. Or could it be, in fact, that the reading material drew café goers?

In truth, I discovered many things going on in the café that could fall under the umbrella of literacy practices—browsing or reading books or magazines; conversations on art, gardening, poetry, or any number of other topics; discussions on recently released books; and just a bit of writing. But I was noticing that for many of the interactions, actual reading material was often peripheral to the tête-à-têtes I observed. It was not uncommon for magazines or books to lie open on laps or pile up on tables only to be ignored or pushed aside if an opportunity for a conversation presented itself. A social phenomenon emerged that began to capture my interest.

As I continued my search for meaning, I wondered whether my interest in literacy would remain a central focus. I needed to fine-tune my thinking and preliminary research questions to reflect what I had been observing. It was time to consider the *why* question noted earlier. Why were folks drawn to the café? What about the café appealed to the patrons? And what about the "frequent flyers"? More than a few often sat in the same locations, and those folks connected with many of the same people. What might be their motivation be for coming back again and again?

I had recognized that more than a few folks gathered there regularly. Perhaps these were the people who would help to explain the café's appeal. One in particular was Jerry, who seemed to "hold court" whenever he arrived. He had the knack of making others feel welcomed. He was genuinely interested in his acquaintances and cordially greeted each one, often with a two-handed hand clasp and a warm smile. It was always, "Great to see you!" or "How have you been?" I later found out he was part of a group that had met a few years previously to discuss individual writing projects. Although the writing group had since disbanded, the relationships remained. The group had continued to share much beyond its writing.

Something about the culture of the café attracted patrons. I became interested in trying to discover why this was so. Yet I was also reluctant to allow my interest in literacy practices to evaporate completely. Might the investigation still be framed around the literacy habits of the patrons? What types of interview questions could address those literacy practices? Since the café was situated in a bookstore, one might assume that café activities would naturally connect to literacy in some way—perhaps previewing books or magazines, discussing recent releases with other café goers, or collecting gift ideas. Or was I working too hard at trying to make literacy the central theme? What types of patterns were emerging that might later prove to be thought-provoking?

I had already spent a bit of time watching people in the bookstore café and had become familiar with typical routines. By positioning myself in different areas, I could nonchalantly eavesdrop on conversations and discovered that topics ranged from family to religion to politics to work to research interests—boundaries appeared to be nonexistent and no topic was off limits. During one particular visit, Jerry, who later emerged as a central character in this story, seemed to be fishing for a worthy topic for the night's discussion with his friends. In the time I was monitoring café activity, the group covered several topics, which included the following: Was the FDA serving Americans the "'right"' way? Do you know anyone in the service? Do you think abortion is right or wrong? Might there be instances in which it would be okay? What do you think about the U.S. position on the war in Iraq? Should capital punishment be allowed? You know that Samson in the Bible killed lots of people, but was it considered "wrong" to do so? When might euthanasia be an acceptable alternative? The rapid-fire topics and the types of questions Jerry posed left me wondering whether he felt it was his mission to promote lively, and sometimes polarizing, conversation. Was this another dimension of the café that was emerging? Could it be that the café provided a backdrop for dialogue where patrons could express opposing opinions in a friendly environment?

I noticed early on that several café characters seemed to stake out territories. Jerry and his friends laid claim to a six-person table located in the middle of the café floor. Over the course of my visits, it was a rare occasion when that middle table was occupied by "foreigners," a term I use to mean those who were not in Jerry's circle of friends. It even became possible to determine the day of the week based on who arrived to join in the typically lively conversations that occurred there. Marty, for instance, was a "Sunday only" visitor due to his hectic work schedule. Jerry called Marty "exquisitely brilliant!," leading me to believe that there was more than a casual relationship between the men. Chuck showed up several times per week, often in the early evening, and was always greeted warmly by the tablemates— "How are those grandkids? And what about your wife? Still working? What do you have there? A petition? Sure, I'll sign it! Good luck!"

Lucky and Jef, on the other hand, were often stationed in the comfy leather chairs that were arranged near the front of the building. They seemed to prefer a vantage point from which all café activity could be observed, and although each brought some form of work to the café, I noted early on that each entertained and obviously welcomed distractions, most often in the form of casual conversation with other patrons. Each took time to reconnect with familiar faces and often relegated work to a back burner.

Dr. Horvat suggested that I investigate the literature that might relate to what I was seeing in order to help me find a worthy *"why"*—to try to understand the meaning in the patterns I was observing. As luck would have it, another Temple University professor had recently examined the coffee shop phenomenon. Bryant Simon's *Everything But the Coffee* looked at Starbucks and suggested that the venue had a "broad and lasting impact on American life" (Simon, 2009, p. 4). What, exactly, was Simon getting at? He suggested that for many, Starbucks met basic needs—it was "a source of entertainment, a strategy for mood management" as well as continuing coffeehouse traditions of the past—as a venue for "connections, conversation, debate and, ultimately, the ongoing and elusive desire for community and belonging in the modern world" (Simon, 2009, p. 82). There was something here worthy of exploring. "Why were people drawn to the café?" could be addressed with Simon's lens—investigated as a unique social phenomenon. There was the potential to uncover and explain reasons that folks were drawn to the café. I continued to look to the literature. Of particular note was a term coined by Ray Oldenburg—*third place*. He refers to "great good places" as "informal public gathering places" (Oldenburg, 1999, p. xviii) that extend beyond the home as first place and work as second. These are places where people of all walks of life are acknowledged and welcomed.

As I took stock of my project, it occurred to me that my focus on literacy practices had shifted from being central to being peripheral. Although literacy practices were apparent—plenty of speaking and listening with some reading and writing mixed in—during all visits to the café, they appeared to be in the service of something quite different. The notion of third place was taking center stage in my investigation. For many, it appeared as if the café was that destination where people sought out both company and conversation.

INTERVIEWING TO INVESTIGATE THE "WHY"

In truth, there was more to be learned from the setting, more than I could ascertain from casual visits and observation. Perhaps collecting thoughts from café patrons would bring clarity to my investigation. A doctoral student observed in Willis (2007), "'Real' qualitative research does not know what the thesis is until the interviews are done and analyzed" (p. 197). Talking to the café patrons might help me understand what I was just beginning to suspect. I was ready to talk to the players.

I crafted what I felt were practical questions that might uncover the reasons why people frequented the café. Were there benefits associated with going to the café? Had I discovered a unique culture that enticed people to return again and again? And was there value in participating in the culture? I hoped that the "'right" questions would help to "identify key issues" (Hesse-Biber & Leavy, 2006, p. 104) that would eventually emerge from and within the site. A winning interview would allow me "to learn about social life through the perspective, experience, and language of those living it" (Hesse-Biber & Leavy, 2006, p. 105) and would undoubtedly contribute to my growing proficiency as a qualitative researcher. Hesse-Biber and Leavy (2006) describe interviewing as a "knowledge producing conversation that occurs between two parties. The relationship between the interviewer and respondent is critical to the process of constructing meaning" (p. 105). Ah! There it was! In my search for meaning, the interview process could likely be the key to a deeper understanding of the drawing power and magic of the café for its patrons! It might elucidate the reasons people frequented the café. If done right, interviewing would allow me to peel back layers of the why question.

An interview protocol began to take shape. I tried to design the interview questions as prompts for a brief conversation of about 15 minutes in length. I needed a framework for initiating an exchange between patrons and me. The first couple of questions were innocuous enough—age (optional), name (pseudonym was acceptable), occupation, family status, among others. I had hoped to dismiss any potential objections by first addressing topics that were safe.

Admittedly, I stumbled through the first couple of interviews. Looking back, I likely explained my intent in more detail than necessary. Most challenging was the approach to initiating an exchange. It was awkward starting conversations with strangers, particularly since I was looking for something from them. One candidate, however, turned out to be extremely helpful as I worked through my jitters. Jef, as noted earlier, was a café regular who preferred sitting in the comfy leather chairs near the front of the café. During one of my visits he became my "prey." I approached with my prepared and too-lengthy introduction. As I spoke, I watched his reaction. Would he willingly engage in a conversation or not? After working through the whole protocol, Jef actually suggested how I might make my initial approach to other café goers less intrusive, yet framed in such a way that information collected during the interview would be meaningful and contribute to my end goal. Jef suggested, "Why don't you say, 'I'm doing a study. Do you mind if I ask a couple of questions?'" That was to the point! My introduction was much more long-winded. I felt folks would appreciate enough background on my project to feel comfortable contributing. I had shared that I was a graduate student working on a research project and that the project required me to gather data at a designated site. I asked if people had the time and whether they were willing to answer some questions, then further explained that all answers would be reported anonymously. Jef, however, sensed that I was saying too much. Might I be overwhelming potentially willing interviewees? I was extremely appreciative and decided to follow his advice with all subsequent conversations. I had refined an introductory script. Next on the agenda was to let the interview protocol guide the next steps of my investigation to "learn about social life through the perspectives, experiences, and language of those living it" (Hesse-Biber & Leavy, 2006, p. 105). The entire interview protocol is included at the end of this chapter.

During the next couple of visits to the café, armed with my list of questions, I sought out willing "victims" to engage. I observed a natural reluctance for customers to make eye contact with me, a stranger, and understood that a conversation might be difficult or uncomfortable for some. This was a challenge to overcome. A dance occurred with café patrons—a brief initial smile that sometimes prompted pleasantries—prior to an actual, substantive conversation. My tactic became to purchase a coffee, thereby blending comfortably into the surroundings, then to select a strategic spot near enough to other café goers so an informal exchange would seem natural. Each visit necessitated examining the environment anew to find a seat where I could talk with as many different people as possible. Things seemed to be in order for making a reasonable stab at gathering data.

While interviewing, I was intent on getting all ideas down on paper as quickly as I could. It is a bit of a challenge to record ideas and think of necessary clarifying questions simultaneously. Tape-recording interviews is often suggested to make the process more manageable. I chose, however, not to record my interviews, thinking it might be too obtrusive. I found myself relying on hasty notes and memory of subjects' responses. Writing up field notes soon after visiting the café was key to having meaningful and robust data. I scheduled time for writing up my reflections within a day of café visits. I paid close attention to using the same set of questions with each of my interview candidates. So I began, and found that most people were genuinely willing and interested in contributing to my data set. A couple of my interview candidates asked how my project was coming along in subsequent visits to the café. And a few people even volunteered friends as worthy subjects. In fact, after his interview, Jef offered, "We can get you lots more people to interview!" with genuine excitement in his voice. I was bolstered by his enthusiasm. Jerry asked more than once to read the final write-up of the study. Although I was willing to share my final project, the bookstore unfortunately closed, making it highly unlikely that I would be able to connect again with the café patrons. I never asked, nor did anyone offer, last names or contact information.

Although it was somewhat awkward invading the personal space of café goers, my initial reluctance to approach strangers was fading. I was aware that my reason for visiting the café was likely different from the reasons that most of the people spent time there. I had assignments to complete; café goers came for other reasons, which would become clearer later as I analyzed my data.

With practice, the interview process became more comfortable. I came to rely less heavily on my scripted questions and was able to glean more from what my interviewees had to say. Clarifying questions became more natural and I began to reflect on different ways to look at my emerging data set. I paid attention to the number of males and females selected as interview candidates since I wondered if gender might matter during my analysis later on. I also paid attention to the ages of respondents so that I would have a cross section. Perhaps responses to interview questions would vary by a subject's age.

As the semester passed, it eventually became time to exit the research site in order to begin data analysis in earnest. But by this time I, too, had become somewhat of a fixture, having made 12 visits and having spent over 24 hours at the café in a few short weeks. My interview pool had grown to 30 participants, many of whom could be considered regulars at the bookstore café. I had become comfortable gathering data to support investigating two questions that emerged: Why did people choose this site as a third place? and What qualities contributed to making the café a third place for people in the area? I had worked through the uncertainties of beginning data collection that were framed by the questions on the Site Selection Prospectus for the class: Who will you be observing? What will you observe? Where will your observations take place? Why will you be observing at this site? Now, I needed to transition to the next part of my journey—making meaning and sense out of the data.

MAKING MEANING THROUGH DATA ANALYSIS

As a novice in the qualitative research world, I wondered about next steps. There were data—actually, more than I knew what to do with—that needed to be organized so that big ideas might emerge. Would the data cluster into meaningful chunks? All that I gathered would likely not be critical to answering my proposed research questions. While interviewing, I had hoped to be able to surface big ideas related to café goers' habits. I had initially wondered about literacy practices that were occurring at the café. Was there something about the café that promoted literacy? What resources in the café supported literacy? These ideas would fade as I began examining data. I wondered if there were specific groups of people who chose to go to the café and why they might visit. These questions would need to be resolved.

I was ready to move forward and looked for some guidance on how to sift through information that I had collected. Although we were encouraged to pause and reflect on data periodically as we wrote field notes, I was uncertain if my reflections to date pointed toward answers to questions I had framed. Perhaps it was time to step back to look more globally at the data. As Dr. Horvat suggests in Chapter 5, I knew I had seen and documented lots of interesting things, but was something important buried in my field notes and would I be able recognize it? What, truly, was *the* meaningful something that I wanted to talk about? I had begun to see some patterns while observing and talking with café customers. There were those for whom the café was truly a regular destination rather than a place they occasionally or randomly visited. As a newcomer to the venue, it quickly became apparent that visits, particularly for the regulars, were intentional. It was clear that the bookstore café offered something special.

At this point, I was just about fully detached from my initial focus on literacy. What had initially drawn me to the bookstore was what I had assumed occurred in bookstores—plenty of reading and other associated literacy activities. Some of the questions I included in the interview protocol might point toward a connection between café visits and literacy practices, but in truth, those associations emerged later on as peripheral. What I had discovered as I continued to focus on just the café area was that much more than literacy-related activities occurred there and that the types of literacy-related activities that did occur did not seem to be the sole impetus for café goers' visits. So why did people choose the café as a third place? The responses seemed to fall into categories that allowed me to propose some reasons for patrons' behavior.

In Chapter 5, Dr. Horvat suggests ways to reflect on data. Since the experience of data collection and reflection was new, I found the guidance more than helpful. During the process of investigating the research site and recording observations through field notes, we were asked to include observer comments (OCs) to help begin making sense of data and to document wonderings. The OCs were a way to talk through points of confusion or make note of things that might prove to be worthy of mulling over later on. They were markers to return to. Memos were also required and were helpful to evaluate progress on our projects.

Along the way, I was not confident that I was on point with wonderings recorded in my memos. Was my analysis of what I thought was happening or what it might mean pointing me in the right direction? Would the way that I chose to look at my data help me understand goings-on at the café? Were the patterns I had noted—people regularly coming to the café and stationing themselves in the same seating areas—merely interesting phenomena, or was there something more meaningful that I would work to uncover? These were the types of questions that helped frame a game plan for data analysis. My next stop was to begin coding!

FOCUSING ON ANALYSIS

How many ways are there to look at data? Professor Horvat suggested that we begin by sorting buttons. Brown? Black? White? Shank? Two-holed? Four-holed? It was difficult to see the connection to my project. In Chapter 5, Dr. Horvat discusses the same idea of "coding" using Halloween candy. Chocolate? Non-chocolate? What I'll keep? What I'll trade? Both sorting buttons and candy seemed to make sense. One can actually see and literally sort concrete objects. Sorting my data, however, was not as clear or simple . . . or so I thought. As is often the case, when you're in the midst of trying to make sense of something, clarity does not come until the end of the journey. I later understood that it was the research questions that governed how I looked at the accumulated information.

I had a fair amount of data that had been collected and analyzed preliminarily in field notes, OCs, and memos. In just a few weeks, I managed to conduct 30 interviews, each about 15 minutes in length, in an attempt to figure out why people frequented the café. But in truth, the amount of narrative was difficult to wade through. I needed to find a way to make the information more manageable so that I could determine if there were, in fact, any connections or patterns that were noteworthy in what I gathered. I had interviews from a purposive sample of café goers that reflected the diversity of the patrons I had seen at the café. I had intentionally selected an equal number of males and females, representing multiple ages. I talked with people in groups as well as with those who preferred to be alone at the café. I approached the regulars and not-so-regulars.

Perhaps a logical starting point might be to look at the data chronologically. Who did I interview first? Next? Last? I had to wonder, however, whether my interview skills had changed, or gotten better or worse over the course of my visits. Was the first interview as clear or comprehensive as the last one? If this was a "real" qualitative research project rather than my initial experience, an experimental data collection period along with analysis would probably have been a good idea. But for the purpose of learning about qualitative research, I had to let go my wonderings about whether or not my data were the "best." I proceeded on.

First, I made a list of all interviewees and noted their ages, occupations, marital status—that was the easy part! As mentioned earlier, I intentionally attempted to select a cross section of the general population as interview candidates—an equal (or close to it) number of males and females with multiple generations represented. Although not a research question, I wondered if either gender or age had anything to do with who frequented the café. I initially thought that people who were regulars at the café might be those with lots of leisure time on their hands—retirees, perhaps? That hunch, as I later discovered through organizing and coding interview responses, was not the case. Next, I had to dive back into my field notes to see how each person responded to the interview questions. This is where my interview competence might make a difference—might there be missing pieces of data? More specifically, did I pose all questions to each candidate? What if there were missing data? Would that undermine the efficacy of the study? Or, more importantly, how would I be able to definitively answer my questions for the project? Admittedly, as a novice, I was unsure if I'd done everything right as I began to organize interview responses. What emerged, however, were similarities among what the interviewees had to say.

EMERGING PATTERNS

Systematically rooting through the data was my next task. Although there are options for sorting data, including software programs, I was perfectly comfortable with a low-tech alternative. I organized all the information in a grid, with candidate demographic information on one side and interview questions as headers across the top of a spreadsheet. With responses in cells, I used colored pencils to code my data. After several reads of each interview, I discovered that many of the answers were close enough in meaning to be able to cluster ideas under larger headings. I began noting similarities, underlining those with the same color—anything having to do with books, I underlined in blue; responses related to friends or meeting people at the café, I underlined in orange. "Meeting friends," "talk with friends," and "friendly people" responses were grouped as social reasons. Replies like "I feel welcomed," "comfortable," and "the warm atmosphere" were coded under ambiance or the character of the café. The "smells in the café" or "more here to do than Starbucks," however, were slightly more challenging to sort out since these responses did not comfortably fit generic categories I was seeing.

The grid began to look like a rainbow and I was on the lookout for the pot of gold. I was searching for meaning that was living and breathing in the data! With all responses color-coded, the next challenge was to create categories or labels for each of the common responses. It was akin to the button and Halloween candy sorting exercises. What larger labels would fit my data? I settled on what seemed to work for my project, although I wasn't sure if I had come up with the "right" labels. Later I discovered that coming up with the label was not the critical part of the exercise; rather, the more important idea was that the information was organized in such a way to point toward possible answers to my research questions. I eventually came up with eight broad categories—Reading, Amenities, Social, Job Related, Location, Café Related, Ambiance or Character, and a final category of Other for those responses that were clearly stand-alones. The pieces were fitting together.

LESSONS LEARNED

What did it take to find meaning at my site? The answer did not come all at once or on schedule, which I would have preferred. Rather, my experience in *doing* qualitative research and searching for meaning was filled with twists and turns. I had spent time collecting data at my site and had interviewed what I felt was a reasonable number of candidates for me to take a stab at addressing my questions—Why did people choose the café as a third place? and What qualities contributed to making the café a third place for people in the area? Now at the end and able to reflect on everything, it is clear that I learned much about the process.

My preconceived notions about qualitative investigations had undergone a transformation. Initial skepticism about the value of conducting research from this perspective gave way to a deeper appreciation of the method. I was able to complete my study within the time frame of a semester's work. There was a beginning, albeit a rocky one, and a well-defined ending to my exploration. I learned to look at data critically and reflectively, almost like an artist turning a piece of work over and over in his hands to examine where refinement needs to occur. My data categories were fluid as I coded responses to my interview questions, working to make each one a reasonable fit that would help me to draw logical conclusions to address my questions. Finally, I learned that *the* answer was not as important as *an* answer, or perhaps rather a reasonable suggestion as to the drawing power of the café.

Additionally, I learned the importance of landing in a site that works for investigation. I had chosen the college library, assuming there would be plenty of activity. Plan B quickly materialized with the café providing everything for a successful initiation into qualitative research. I guess the possibility exists that site #2 could have also turned belly-up, which is why flexibility and stamina will serve the novice qualitative researcher well.

Entering a site is fraught with uncertainty. What are you looking for? What might be important to note? What kind of data should you collect? What is significant in the data-gathering process? Dr. Horvat addresses these concerns in detail in the following chapter. However, an important idea here is that at the beginning, it is difficult to know what you might need to get to the end of your journey successfully. So take it all in. No matter how insignificant a detail or conversation might seem in the moment, make note of it. For instance, I noticed early on that there were "frequent flyers" at the café. Their presence turned out to be more than coincidental. Rather, their visits were planned and predictable. One, Jerry, visited the café at least 5 days a week but always left close to dinnertime. Lucky came every weekday early in the afternoon and spent at least 2 hours doing crosswords and catching up with friends. It was through observations and talking to these people that I was able to frame questions for my investigation, ending in a very different place than where I'd initially intended.

Put careful thought into creating your interview and with an eye toward zeroing in on data that could contribute to your study. The list of questions provided a framework for my conversations and kept me on course. It allowed me to avoid rabbit trails or dead ends. However, I found that an occasional derailing was what allowed me to experience the café as a third place. Much was shared outside the boundaries of the interview questions that did not impact my study. This sharing among new friends was one of the highlights of my research study. I found out about Jerry's family and how proud he was of his daughter and grandkids. I discovered Art's continuing passion to stay connected to performance, both as an actor and director. I watched

Ray collect signatures from supporters so that he could run for local office. I learned that Christian was a foreign student who used the café as not only a place to study but also to learn about other people and the American culture. Ann, a schoolteacher, shared that she was extremely shy and her visits to the café supported her need to experience social environments. And Nicole, a regular visitor for at least 6 years, indicated that the café was her home away from home and a place for multi-generational interactions. I found out about people's lives.

Next, take time to reflect and wonder along the way. In the busyness of a class or a project, deadlines often dominate. However, it is well worth the time to take stock of what you've noticed and to wonder about where you might be headed. For me, I had committed to visiting my site for several hours each week. Afterward, I dutifully documented observations and conversations. Part of this was straightforward: "When I was at the café this week, I noticed that Patrick typically sits alone, yet he makes rounds through the café to reconnect with his friends, from baristas to other café goers," or "Jerry thinks that conversations with friends are what keep him coming back." What I could have missed was stopping to document the feel of the place. As it turned out, the atmosphere of the café, an intangible, was a key idea for many of the café patrons. They enjoyed their time there because of the way it made them feel. The ambiance of the place drew them back again and again.

Next, when all the data are analyzed, don't be surprised if the analysis takes you in an unexpected direction. I was initially intent on looking at literacy practices of café goers and was reasonably confident that those practices would abound in a bookstore café. It was a comfortable place where people could not only read but also talk about their reading with one another. What I found was that although the café patrons seemed interested in conversations about reading, they were equally or perhaps even more motivated to visit the café to nurture relationships with others. More than a few came to the café to develop and maintain friendships. In his discussion of third places, Oldenburg (1999) mentions that community is important to human social, emotional, and cognitive experiences. The café provided that community. It was the quality of the interactions and the relationships that developed within the context of the café that were meaningful for many patrons.

And, finally, know that it's acceptable to tweak your research questions along the way. It wasn't until after I did a bit more research into social phenomena and the notion of *third places* that I finally landed on what proved to be a worthy (at least from my perspective!) research study. I was able to find meaning at the site through both my observations and talking to people who spent time there.

INTERVIEW PROTOCOL*

1. What is your name? A pseudonym is acceptable.
2. How old are you?
3. What is your current occupation?
4. Describe your educational background.
5. Are you married? Single?
6. Do you live nearby?
7. Can you tell me why you come here?
8. How frequently do you visit the café and bookstore? Are you a morning or afternoon visitor? Typically a weekday or weekend visitor?
9. Why do you like it here?
10. In your opinion, what makes the café comfortable? Welcoming?
11. Do you drink coffee?
12. Out of all the local coffee shop choices, why do you come here?
13. If this café wasn't here, where would you go?
14. Is visiting this café a planned part of your day? Do you set out to come here? Or do you stop by only when in the neighborhood?
15. Is visiting the cafe a solitary or social event for you?
16. Would you like to ask me a question?

*Note that the interview questions were intended only to guide my inquiry. Some prompted more revealing and interesting responses than others.

Part II

FIELDWORK

CHAPTER THREE

Ethnographic Eyes
Developing a Qualitative Project

Erin Horvat

Often at the start of my course students will come to the class or my office hours having spent one or maybe two sessions observing at their research site and say, "There is nothing to see." It is obvious that they also want to say, "This is a colossal waste of time." They are dispirited and suspicious. All of this—observing at the site, writing field notes, and so forth—takes so much time, and they are concerned that they will not be able to *show* anything. Especially if they are observing in a classroom, students will say something like, "Well, there is not much going on. The students are at their desks or engaging in various activities at learning centers around the room and the teacher is teaching. There isn't anything to see." They begin to question the whole approach. How can you learn something from just watching people? The answer to this question, of course, lies in what and how one watches.

We observe or watch people all the time. We have been doing it from birth. We watch our world so that we know what to do. As children, we watch parents and family members and learn how to interact. As we head out into the world we watch peers and teachers, the people on the street and those who float in and out of our lives (the mail carrier, the checker at the grocery store, the doctor, dentist, ice cream vendor, other kids at the playground, etc.). Watching others is how we learn how to "be" in the world.

This watching is second nature to us. We do not necessarily know that we are doing it. The famous sociologist Erving Goffman spent much of his career making explicit the implicit ways in which the unwritten rules of social interaction are acted out in public. As Goffman notes, "In all societies, rules of conduct tend to be organized into codes which guarantee that everyone acts appropriately. . . ." (Goffmann, 1967, p. 55). Goffman calls these rules a set of codes, ceremonial and substantive, and notes that the ceremonial expressions and rules are part of etiquette, where these social rules are explicitly stated. Goffman also makes the point that these rules are context-bound. He is interested not in "men and their moments. Rather moments and their men" (p. 3). Thus the moment, the social context, is critical to the set of rules that govern social interaction.

We watch others and "automatically" process what we see so that we can operate in the world without "thinking" about every interaction and still be able to navigate through the world. Athletes, musicians, and others often talk about the way in which they do not consciously think about what they are doing when they are performing. A baseball player unconsciously reads a batter and shifts position to be able to stop a line drive. A musician in an experienced ensemble adjusts to others as a piece unfolds. Often these performers will talk about mistakes, fielding errors, or discordant sounds as moments when they "overthought" what they were doing. These performers are in a state of "flow," where they unconsciously perform at high levels (Csikszentmihalyi, 1997). These moments occur in daily life as well. Normally, we effortlessly navigate down busy sidewalks or hallways without running into one another. And yet there are moments where we may overthink the interaction and wind up "dancing" with an oncoming person. Our reactions to much of the incoming stimuli are automatic. We have an internal sense of the rules governing our social interaction and we do not consciously think about most of our responses to others or our environment.

We make sense of our world so completely that we do not even think about these millions of micro-interactions. And yet it is these interactions that make up the patterns of behavior we are usually interested in observing. So the task for the beginner qualitative researcher is to learn to see the world in a new way—to see in a way that makes explicit all of the implicit sense-making and resulting actions of people in social contexts.

So, let's return to my students who return from their first site visit claiming there is nothing to see. The teacher is just teaching and the students are just being students. What does this mean? What does it mean to teach in this classroom? Lecturing from the front of the room or leading an active class discussion? Does it result in learning? How do you know? The students are just being students. What does it mean to be a student in this particular classroom? Developing the ability to see beyond or rather *into* these routine interactions and understand what they mean is to develop an ethnographic eye.[1] In order to see the meaning in a situation, context, or interaction, to understand why or whether or not it is important, and to suspend our automatic sense-making judgment regarding what this action means, the researcher needs to develop the ability to see the meaning in the implicit routine interactions of daily life at the research site.

One of the keys to understanding the meaning of observable actions and interactions is to understand that all action is situated in a specific context. Again, this is something we have been learning since we were very young children. As any child will tell you, the rules or norms for interaction at home are different than they are for school or the playground. From the very first mention of "inside voices" and "dress-up clothes" we learn very early on that one does not wear his or her holiday clothes to a barbeque and that screaming at the top of your lungs is okay on the playground but not in the classroom. Context matters. As many others have pointed out (Bourdieu, Goffman), it is the context that in part helps determine the appropriateness of actions in a particular social setting. Different social worlds have different rules of interaction.

When I was in graduate school I developed what my husband would call an "unhealthy interest" in etiquette books. I was riveted by Miss Manners (Judith Martin) and picked up old copies of Emily Post with glee at yard sales. Far from using these guides to advance my social standing, I was fascinated by the way that they made explicit the accepted norms of interactions in different contexts. The rules for social interaction varied across space and time and these writers revealed when and how they changed and often what the rules meant. The accepted methods for expressing a romantic interest in another person vary greatly from the 1952 Emily Post classic to the mid-1980s Miss Manners version. And now in 2013, Google, Facebook, and JDate have changed it all again.

For a girl like me, raised in Southern California where the "rules" were rather loose, especially when it came to fashion, Emily Post's explication of the importance of footwear and handbags as a signal of social class to Manhattanites in the 1950s was riveting. It allowed me to peer into another world, to understand the signals, language, and customs of others. To wear white after Labor Day (mostly on the East Coast) was not simply a fashion misstep, it was an indication that one did not know the rules or speak the language of a certain context. These texts reveal the language and rules of certain classes during certain eras in given contexts.

So what does this "unhealthy interest" in etiquette have to do with advancing scholarly knowledge by watching people? Rather than seeing these etiquette books as rules to follow to someday merit an entry in the Social Register, I saw them as field guides to another world. The ability to develop an ethnographic eye, to understand the meaning of social miscues and rules, allows the qualitative researcher to see inside the social interaction. It means that the person watching understands (or is trying to understand or beginning to understand) the meaning behind the actions. Diving into your dinner before your hostess has begun her meal is not just "bad manners." It is also a signal that the eager diner does not operate by the same social rules. While breaking some social rules (using the wrong fork, wearing white before Memorial Day, etc.) are simply social or fashion faux pas, attending to or breaking other social rules carries great weight and meaning. It may tell a potential mother-in-law that you're not refined enough to be part of her family. The weight and import of these social rules explains why diplomats are trained extensively in the customs of the country they are visiting. It is the ethnographer's job to develop a "field guide view" of their site that provides an understanding of the implicit rules that govern social interaction. This understanding of the context will be directed and limited by the interest of the researcher and her question. So how do you begin to develop an ethnographic eye? The first thing to think about is what to watch followed closely by thinking about how you watch. Over time you will develop an ethnographic sensibility, a way of seeing the world, as well as the requisite skills to make the implicit meanings of social worlds explicit.

HOW DO I BEGIN COLLECTING DATA?

Similar to the observational exercise from the Chapter 1, you will have many questions and concerns as you enter the field. You will likely experience uncertainty and some trepidation as you begin. Much of this uncertainty and fear is related to not knowing exactly what to do in the field.

As you develop an ethnographic eye, how do you go about actually collecting data? What do you do? How do you do field notes? How do you decide what to watch? How do you decide where to position yourself? How do you conduct an interview? Where do you come up with the questions? Do you write them down? The way in which you, as a researcher, answer or respond to these questions will shape the field guide that you develop of your site. What you choose to focus on and how you choose to do it will influence what you see and study. Remember: It depends.

At some sites it makes sense to talk with key informants first to get oriented to the site while at other places it would be better to just watch for a while to even figure out who the key informants are. You will have to feel your way. Generally speaking, I suggest to students that they observe for a while before beginning to talk with people. You can learn a lot by watching and thinking about what you are seeing. After some time watching and learning you will likely ask better questions of informants at the site and be able to develop better interview questions. So the first thing to do is to watch—watch and take field notes.

FIELD NOTES:
WHAT ARE THEY AND WHAT IS SO HARD?

Field notes are, simply, the written record of your observations at your site. That's it. So what's so hard? Well, students who take my qualitative research methods class have to turn in field notes every week. They visit their site every week, write field notes, and turn them in. For me as an instructor, reading the students' notes took a good deal of time. Once I felt that they had learned the craft, why did I continue to make them turn them in? I learned that if I didn't, the students often stopped doing them and fell behind. Some actually asked me to *require* them to turn in their notes; otherwise they could not make themselves complete them. The requirement forced them to stay on top of this task. Why is it so hard to keep up with field notes? What could be so frustrating about writing up your notes? Why do they take so long? The answer is, they take so much time and they are frustrating because, especially at the beginning, you do not know what to write down. But they are critical to your research. Let me say that again: They are critical to your research. So what is so hard about field notes?

More Is More

As Pat McDonough, one of my research mentors, once told me, more is more. While this may be an unpopular minority opinion, longer field notes are generally better. That is not to say that 30 pages of uninsightful text are useful. But it is true that the way we collect these data about others is by writing down what we see and hear. If you do not record your observations and your insights about them, then you do not have data. If you write down lots of observations and take time to explore their meaning for your study and the site, you will have more data. More is usually more (and better) when it comes to field notes. It is also true that at the beginning of a project the researcher is often not sure what is important at the site and so it is important to write down as much as possible.

There is no substitute for going to your site for a couple of hours, writing your notes in longhand on a small unobtrusive notepad or, if appropriate for your site, taking rough notes on your laptop or tablet computer, going immediately home, and writing your field notes. When you are at the site you are recording as much of what you see and hear as possible. Can you get verbatim quotations of critical conversations? Can you describe what the people and place look, feel, and smell like? Capture as much of this in a shorthand that will make sense to you later as you can and then head to your computer right after leaving your site. Take your handwritten or typed rough first draft notes and plan to spend two to three times as long as you were in the field writing them up. You will use your rough notes to jog your memory of events, and you'll use your memory to flesh out the notes in colorful detail. Don't wait more than a few hours to turn these rough notes into polished field notes. Your memory of the events will erode quickly, making the notes harder to write and usually less detailed.

Along the way, while you are writing these notes you will add in "Observer Comments." Observer comments are your thoughts on what you are seeing. Why was a particular interaction interesting? What intrigues you about what you are seeing? What question came up in your mind as you were observing? You will write these in your notes in some way that differentiates them from the who, what, when, and how aspect of your field notes. Some people type their observer comments in italics or bold while others create a two-column format for their field notes. The method you develop for recording your observer comments is irrelevant and you will likely develop a method that works for you. But the idea of keeping track of what happened and what you think of what happened is key. This all sounds pretty straightforward, right? So why is this so hard? Well, in my case it is complicated by the fact that I never learned to type properly. I do a wicked fast hunt and peck that is not even close to being as fast as a mediocre typist using good technique. So the notes are more tedious for me than they might be had I paid attention in 8th-grade typing class. Beyond that personal failing, I find field notes both exhilarating and exhausting. They are exhilarating because of the way they enable you to learn about social worlds and exhausting because they take so much time and energy.

Fieldwork takes energy. It takes energy to carefully watch and make sense of what you are seeing. Think about what it feels like to be on the first day of a new job or in the first week as a foreign-exchange student. In both cases you are working very hard to understand the new world in which you find yourself, just like our friend Arnie in 1st grade, from Chapter 1. It is draining, exciting, and interesting at the same time. As you begin to understand the world you are observing you are trying to understand the implicit rules of interaction by capturing detail in your notes. Focusing that intensely for 2 to 3 hours at a time while at the same time being somewhat unsure of which interactions or moments will be important to your research question takes patience and energy.

Then, after all of this watching, I have to keep up a head of steam long enough to write out these detailed notes that require me to draw on my memory of the events. It is exhilarating when I see something that I think is important or figure out some special dynamic at my site. It is just great when I get a real verbatim quotation that bears directly on my research question. This does not happen on every site visit. And when field notes are not exhilarating, they are boring. Yup, boring. Monotonous, too. When it is just another day in the field and you are seeing events similar to what you have seen before and you have to take time to write them up in excruciating detail over and over again, it can get boring and monotonous. However, it is in this boring and monotonous work that you will find the detail that will make your research, well, research. Capturing in vivid detail the inner workings of a group or interaction takes time. As qualitative researchers we are usually looking for patterns that reveal meaning. The quotes and excerpts that make it into our articles and books are exemplars—really good examples of a larger phenomenon or pattern of activity. In order to understand the pattern or the phenomenon, we need to document it—hence field notes.

In addition to resenting the energy it takes to write good field notes, I hate the monotony of field notes. I also hate that it takes so darn long to do them. I have other things to do. This is one of the problems with fieldwork in general. It takes time, so much of it. It can be hard to fit it in with your life. As my commitments to others have grown (a real job, husband, children, ailing relatives, etc.) it has become harder and harder to do fieldwork myself. As a result, I have at times resorted to what my friend and colleague Annette Lareau calls "remote control ethnography," where I direct a project with others doing the bulk of the fieldwork. While this has, at times, been a necessity for me it is always a less than satisfying experience as I have less direct contact with the site and study participants. In my case it is an unhappy bargain that I have made. I think the projects have turned out fine. We have learned something worth knowing and some graduate students have learned how to do good fieldwork. But on balance I think studies turn out better when the principal investigator is doing a good bit of the data collection (field notes and interviews).

Finally, I find field notes challenging because I also find it difficult to emotionally engage with people at the site and to then reengage (mentally and emotionally) with them while I write up the notes. When I write field notes and everyone is different, and every project is different, I replay the scenes from the site in my mind as I write the notes. It is almost like a movie running in my head. As I usually study inequality, it is often painful to replay and reexperience these sometimes distressing moments where opportunity and access are lost in schools. I might feel differently if I were studying more uplifting topics. But for me the mental and emotional replay required while writing field notes is painful and draining. The older I get the less patience I have for it. Yet the more experience I have as a qualitative researcher, the more important I know that good field notes are. They are the heart and soul of a study.

What Do I Watch? What Do I Write Down?

It can also be difficult to know where to focus when you are collecting data. This is very true at the beginning of a study. I use the images of a vacuum cleaner and a spotlight[2] to help students understand what to focus on in their study. At the start of the study I suggest that the researcher think about functioning like a vacuum cleaner. Vacuum cleaners indiscriminately suck up everything they come across—dirt, small bugs, safety pins, a diamond that has fallen out of the setting of a ring. It does not matter what it is, up it goes. The same is true for a researcher starting out at her site. While the beginning researcher may have some idea of what she may be focusing on, it is usually a fairly loose idea. This loose idea does not allow the researcher to discriminate. It is difficult to tell at this point in the journey whether something that is hard and smooth in spots is a diamond or a safety pin. As the study progresses and the researcher develops a better idea of what the study is about, it becomes easier to discriminate. At this point, when you can tell the difference between a diamond and a safety pin, you can choose what to focus on and ignore things you know are not relevant, like bugs and dirt. Eventually the researcher becomes like a spotlight shining its focus on areas of interest, scooping up all of the "diamonds" she finds.

So what, aside from length, makes for good field notes? Colorful detail is one thing: Most good ethnographic studies are filled with detail. They are, in this respect, journalistic. The reader is left with a sense of who these people in the study are after reading the account. We can bring up an image in our mind's eye of the people about whom we have read. Good notes have detailed descriptions of the people, place, and process of importance at the site. Below is an excerpt of a field note that covers about 20 minutes of observation from a student who was observing in a high school library. The note that appears below is a "polished" field note. The student started with the rough notes he had taken at the site. Using his memory and these rough notes he produced the text you see below.

> Harold is on the phone. He speaks in a choppy, muddled, deep voice that is hard to make out even from a short distance. He appears to be looking for someone. He finds another aide, Elle, a middle-aged woman with a limp, a curious scar on her lip, and her blond hair cut that is unusually short in length. Harold says something indistinguishable and then returns to the phone. Pat blows her nose. A student volunteer, young girl with glasses, paces back and forth. Harold is wearing a long-sleeved blue dress shirt tucked into a pair of khakis, supported by a brown belt. He is tall, over 6 feet and an imposing yet awkward figure. He sports large, old-fashioned glasses. His hairline has receded or is at least placed strangely back on his head. His shoulders are bulky and carried high up near his neck. He stands stiffly upright. There is something Herman Munsterish about him in build and gait. A student inquires about a library fine. Harold looks it up for her on the computer and moves on to another student. A girl impatiently taps her fingers on the counter, waiting to be attended to. An African American[3] girl with glasses leans forward trying to see the computer screen. She smiles but looks nervous.

> Three male students now pile in line. A skinny African American girl sidles up and butts in line. She looks flustered. She's making arm motions, raising her hand and scowling at Trish as she frantically tries to handle the growing line of students. In a flash, there are all of a sudden over 10 people in line. Trish is yelling for Sandy, another librarian. Total chaos. The line continues to extend. It's all hands on deck. Lillian and Sandy arrive to assist Harold and Trish. A young Hispanic male with an earring bounces up and down as he is served. The line is now back 20 plus students. They are close to backing up to the turnstiles near the entrance.

Usually good field notes are done immediately after leaving the site. Right after leaving the site you will be able to recall in better detail the people and place. The farther you get away from that experience the more your memory erodes. My opinion is that if field notes are not completed within 48 hours of leaving the site their value is greatly diminished. I might not even include them as data in the study. If I did I would label them differently than other field notes, as more suspect material. It is never a good idea to fall behind on your notes. If one set is not finished I think long and hard about going back into the field (and collecting yet more data in rough field note form) before finishing them.

Good field notes are also relevant to the question that is guiding the study. They provide insight into the phenomenon or people you want to learn something about and be able to say something about. This may sound obvious. However, as will be explained in greater detail by Bradley Bergey in Chapter 6, settling on your research question or object for study is not always as easy and straightforward as it first appears. Use your field notes to refine your focus and move closer to an answerable question.

One of the other reasons that I dislike field notes is that to write good ones the researcher must take her own positionality into account. That is, in doing field notes one's own positionality vis-à-vis the topic and people one is watching needs to become explicit. As Emily Tancredi-Brice Agbenyega notes in the following chapter, it requires the researcher to lay bare her own biases and interests about a topic. This requires some level of introspection and self-awareness. Doing this introspection and being explicitly aware of oneself also take time and energy.

INTERVIEWS: WHEN, WHY, AND HOW

Some students want to start talking to people right away. Others find the prospect of actually talking to people at their site frightening and postpone it as long as possible. Should you talk to lots of people or only a

few? How long should the interviews be? Do you need a detailed protocol? Should you tape-record your interviews? Guess what—it depends.
Sometimes researchers talk with people informally. Usually these conversations have to do with what is happening in the moment. They are generally not audio-recorded and do not follow a particular protocol. Some
formal interviews are brief, 15 minutes or less. Usually, if the interviews
are this brief there are many of them. Sometimes what is called for are
several in-depth interviews with a few key individuals over the course of
the study. Usually the researcher writes down some of the questions he
wants to ask beforehand. Sometimes there is a detailed interview protocol
with specific questions and other times there are a few key questions and
the interviewer lets the interview take its course from there. Usually interviews that are planned in advance with a set time and location are audio-
recorded. However, it depends on the nature of the site and the nature of
what the researcher is trying to learn about. The studies my students have
done that have had many brief interviews include Mary Lou Heron's study
from Chapter 2 as well as another conducted by a student who wanted
to understand how high school students experienced detention. She conducted brief interviews with several students in detention. Other students
who have conducted longer interviews or multiple interviews with several
people include a student who studied a small dance class over the course
of a semester and focused on a few participants closely, and a student who
studied teachers who worked together in a small self-contained classroom,
focusing on how their relationships influenced their work. The kind of
interviews you do and the tools you use to do them (interview protocol,
audio recorder, notepad) vary from one study to the next depending on the
research question and site context.

There is also a difference between informal interviews that happen on
the spur of the moment at a site and formal, even brief, interviews. These informal interviews or chats happen while you are observing and are critically
different from interviews that are set in advance or driven by a protocol (a
detailed list of questions asked in a specific order developed by the researcher). It is not uncommon to strike up a conversation with someone at the
site and before you know it you are asking interview-type questions. This is
normal and often quite useful, but it is not exactly the same as an interview.
It has the advantage of being at times more relaxed and the interviewer/
researcher has the opportunity to ask questions *in situ*—that is, in the context
of the field site. At times this may result in more genuine, unguarded conversations. The disadvantage is that it may also result in conversations that are
less reflective than in a formal interview. The responses may also be more
guarded if the respondent is concerned that she may be overhead. Often the
researcher will not have the opportunity to record these conversations or it

may be awkward to do so. Valuable data can be lost. There are drawbacks and advantages to various strategies.

Selecting the best time to interview also depends on several factors. Sometimes it can be good to talk with key informants early on in the study in order to get the lay of the land. Often, though, I find it better to wait until I understand something of the site before talking with people. I have better questions and have usually developed some rapport with participants at the site. I also worry that with some folks, I may only get one chance to talk with them. People are busy. Often I am wary of "wasting" an interview opportunity by doing it too early, but I also do not like to hold all interviews until too late in the project. Ideally, I like to have a nice back-and-forth with interviews and observations. I like to gain an initial understanding of the site through observation, interview some people, return to the site with the knowledge gained from the interviews, and then do more interviews later. It does not always work out this way and there are studies where this kind of back-and-forth is not possible, but for me it is often ideal if the observations and interviews inform one another.

I love interviews. They offer an opportunity to see inside the social world or process I am interested in learning about. For me it feels like a reward for all of that time spent in the field (writing those darn field notes!) prior to interviewing. It feels like opening a present. I can finally talk with people at the site about what I have been seeing and hearing. I can often test out ideas and assumptions. Good interviewees can describe in detail a process or instance that has meaning for me and my research.

I also love talking to people. I love talking to people so much that it is sometimes a problem. This is because interviews are different from normal conversations. In a normal, routine conversation there is usually a relatively equal exchange of information: "How was your day? Fine. How was yours? Great." There are, of course, times when we listen more and talk less in normal conversations, such as when a friend calls us with a problem. And of course we all know people who consistently talk more than they listen, broadcasting their concerns to the world. But in general we talk and listen with relatively equal frequency in the course of a conversation.

An interview is not a normal conversation. The point of this conversation is to gather information from the interviewee, not get to know one another as people. Thus the "rules" of the conversation are different. Rather than the usual back and forth where we share information and experiences, the conversation ought to be much more one-sided. Rather than seeking that normal conversational balance where you listen to the person and then share back an experience or reaction of your own, you seek to affirm the interviewee's contribution and encourage more. This means that rather than replying to the interviewee with a comparable story, instance, or reply, such as

"Oh, I had a similar experience once . . ." or "I felt the same way when . . . ," instead you smile, nod, and ask a question about the experience that the interviewee just shared. There should be far more of the interviewee's voice on your recording than yours.

As I said, I love talking to people. This is an asset in that I can chat easily with people and usually establish rapport with a stranger rather quickly. However, I am also burdened by a desire for the other to know that I understand them. For me, it is not enough to say "I understand." I want to *show* them I understand. Early in my interviewing career, I did this by finishing people's sentences for them. This tendency to finish others' sentences is merely annoying for my husband and children. In a research situation it was a disaster. Rather than having the juicy quote from the participant on the tape, I had my voice filling in the best parts. Almost always I was right. That is, I was correctly finishing the sentence. I understood the dilemma or ideas the interviewee, God bless them, was trying to get across, if only I would have let them. As Seidman instructs (2013), listen more and talk less. Your job is not to convince the interviewee that you get it, that you understand their experience, though this can be useful to build rapport. Rather, your job is to make the interviewee as comfortable as possible and ask really good questions, follow them up with more good questions, and listen actively to what the interviewee is saying.

So what does it mean to listen actively? First it means to pay attention. Often when we listen to others our minds are elsewhere, thinking about what we are going to have for dinner, whether we forgot to let the dog out, or whether or not we like the other person's scarf. If you are actively listening, your mind is actively engaged with what the other person is saying to you. You are hearing what he is saying and thinking about it as he talks. You are thinking about how it fits with what you have learned already and what you might want to hear more about. You might be thinking about how the other person feels about what she is saying to you. The point is that it is not normal everyday listening. It is deeper, more attentive, and takes a lot more energy. It helps you to listen actively and in interviewing in general if you actually *do* have an intense curiosity about what the other person is saying. If you are genuinely riveted by what someone is telling you, it is easier to listen actively. If you are not genuinely interested, fake it. You may become interested by feigning interest. In my experience, if you really do want to hear more (or pretend to really want to hear more), you will ask good follow-up questions and the interviewee will generally open up.

In addition to being an active listener there are many other good rules of the road that you can learn. I use Seidman's (2013) very nice little book on interviewing in my class. He has a chapter that summarizes the key skills of interviewing. While I recommend the book in its entirety, the section headings from the chapter covering interview technique provide as good an overview as any of the do's and don'ts of interviewing. My favorites include:

- Listen More, Talk Less
- Follow Up on What the Participant Says
- Ask Questions When You Don't Understand
- Ask to Hear More About a Subject
- Explore, Don't Probe
- Listen More, Talk Less, and Ask Real Questions
- Avoid Leading Questions
- Ask Open-Ended Questions
- Follow Up, Don't Interrupt
- Ask Participants to Tell You a Story
- Keep Participants Focused and Ask for Concrete Details
- Ask Participants to Reconstruct, Not Remember
- Explore Laughter
- Follow Your Hunches
- Tolerate Silence

In his book Seidman provides detail on each of these directives. Here I clarify a few. When he suggests that researchers should be asking "real questions," he means that they should be asking questions to which they do not already know or anticipate the answer. He also makes the very good point that asking people to reconstruct is asking them to tell what happened rather than to relate their memory of what happened. By suggesting that interviewers explore laughter Seidman suggests that laughter can either mask or amplify something that the participant has to say. By exploring an interviewee's laughter we can attempt to understand the meaning behind the laughter.

INTERVIEW RULES OF THE ROAD: NUTS AND BOLTS

In addition to these tips on how to conduct a good interview, there are other nuts-and-bolts issues that warrant mention. So below are my "rules of the road" for interviewing.

Always Record the Interview When Possible

Some people rely on interview notes. I do not find this to be a useful strategy. While I may take notes during an interview, these are usually to remind me to follow up on a specific point or to return to a topic. I find it almost impossible to pay close attention—that is, to actively listen—to an interviewee and take notes at the same time. Thus, recording the interview is essential for me. There are some situations when it is impossible to record an interview. There can be times when participants do not want to have their voice recorded, where it would be awkward to record the interview or impractical to do so. However, whenever possible I find it is usually best to record interviews.

Make Sure You Are Happy with the Space Where the Interview Will Take Place

What do I look for in an interview space? The first prerequisite for a good space for interviewing is that the participant and I will be able to talk freely, without worrying who may overhear our conversation. Thus, I am usually looking for a small office or room with a door that we can close. The second is that the audio-recording equipment will be able to pick up our voices. A space with too much background noise can create very frustrating recordings. It can be hard to hear the voices over the din of the background. Digital recorders are so good now that recording in cafés and restaurants is generally workable, but be sure to verify that you can make out the important voices on the recording before going too far in the interview. Also, be sure that the interviewee will be able to talk in a candid manner in a public space. Last, the interview space should be one where the interviewee is as comfortable as possible. I generally try to interview people on their own "turf." I try to let the interviewee select the place and often interview individuals at their home or office. I believe that this is more comfortable for the interviewee. It also allows me to see their home or office, another potentially useful data collection opportunity. It takes a good bit of time and energy to conduct and transcribe an interview. I try to make sure the conditions are ideal in order to maximize this effort.

Write a Protocol Before Interviewing Anyone

While it is tempting to just start talking to people and see where the interview goes, I am usually much happier when I have given the interview sufficient thought prior to sitting down with someone. I like to have a detailed protocol—a detailed list of questions developed by the interviewer prior to the interview—written that I follow closely or use as a rough guide during the interview. My approach (whether the protocol is loose or tightly scripted) varies from one study to the next and from one point in a study to another. It depends.

Check, Double-Check, and Have Backup

I think of interviews as high-stakes events in the life of a study. To have someone meet with you at a preset time, at a preset, carefully selected location, and to have that person's attention for 30 to 90 minutes is a significant investment. I always check and double-check everything to make sure the interview will go well. Did I record the time and location of our meeting correctly? I usually send an e-mail or call the day before the interview to confirm our appointment. Is my recording equipment working? Do I have backup equipment and extra batteries? Do I have a copy of the interview protocol? A pen, paper, business cards, et cetera? Do I know how to get where I need to go? What about parking? Taking care of these details, arriving early at the interview to make sure the selected site will work and that you will not be late, will allow you to relax and focus on the interview. Checking equipment and making sure that everything possible has been done to ensure the interview goes well is important.

Show Appreciation

When someone spends time talking with you as a part of your study it is a gift, even if you are paying them. Treat it as such. They are generously sharing their time, energy, and insights with you, a relative stranger. Be gracious and thank them verbally. It is often appropriate to bring a small treat, such as food or drink, to the interview (donuts and coffee in the morning, a small cake or pie, etc.). Always write a formal, heartfelt brief note of thanks following the interview. While you may have said thank you in person, nothing replaces a formal written thank-you note. If a thank-you note is not appropriate in a given setting, or there are barriers to participants reading such a note (lack of an address for a homeless person, inability to read, etc.), determine what act would constitute a formal expression of gratitude and do it.

ROLE MANAGEMENT

Every time I teach my class, a few students ask me if they can conduct their study where they work. Many of my students work in schools and they want to make all of this observing and note taking work with their busy schedules. They also know that they can gain access to their own school or organization. Sadly, I tell almost all of them that it is not a good idea. Why, you ask? The short answer is that it is too complicated. The longer answer builds on this idea of "it's complicated" by talking with students about how hard it is to see a familiar place with "fresh" (ethnographic) eyes; how challenging it can be to manage their role as a researcher at the site, including figuring out what to say about what they are doing and what to promise people at the site about their results; and finally how to manage relationships and insights during the research process.

The experience of a student we will call Rob illustrates many of the ways in which it is too complicated to observe where you work. Rob is a teacher at a middle school. He also coaches sports after school and has a growing family—he is a busy guy. But Rob wants to learn how to collect qualitative data. He has heard it is a lot of work but figures that if he can find a way to observe where he works, he can find time to get his hours in during his free time at work.

When we meet to discuss his site Rob tells me that his school is big and he usually does not leave his corner of the second-floor wing where he works with his special education students. He wants to observe in the library—a part of the school he has only been to once or twice. He reasons that if he uses his prep period and his lunch he will be able to "get in his hours." Usually I am firm with students that they must find a place to observe that is new to them. I want them to have the experience of gaining access to the site. I also have found, over the years, that it is hard for students to have any perspective on a place that they have frequented before. I have learned that managing the role of being a participant observer is hard enough without also having to disentangle oneself from the other role the individual has in the organization. But, given that Rob does not know the librarians, has only been in the library twice, and is a convincing salesman on his choice of site, I allow him to conduct his mini-ethnography at the library in the school where he works. I may have been swayed by the fact that Rob intended to "contain" his observations to the social world of the library, even though I know that as a place in a school community the boundaries of this world would be fuzzy and likely at times include people and events that are beyond its technical borders. Rob's Site Selection Prospectus was approved by me despite some nagging misgivings. Rob also easily got approval from the librarians and school principal and began his mini-ethnography in good form. It did not take long, however, for role management issues to crop up. In his second field note Rob notes the following in an observer comment after being "recognized" by one of his students and interrupted from his scheduled observations:

> The hazards of conducting a study in my own school are on full display. I had literally observed for 2 minutes before this interruption. I'm grateful as anything for this experience however since my future research will also likely be conducted in this same school. My feeling, upon reflection, is that if I end

up being a participant observer at times, then so be it. However, the dual roles of participant/observer and plain observer are something I will have to frequently negotiate and I need to remain aware of the issue.

Not only was Rob learning how to observe, deciding where to look, learning how to get down the detail and nuance required in field notes; but he continually had to fend off requests of himself as a teacher and professional in the building to help out or weigh in on things when all he wanted to do was watch what was happening at the library. He also had to learn how to manage his role as a teacher at this site and his newer role and less familiar role as a researcher.

Will you be able to see the goings-on at the site with "ethnographic eyes," seeing the meaning in the mundane details if you work there? Will you be able to manage the dual role you will have at the site of participant (teacher, coworker, etc.) and observer/researcher? How will you do this? When students start out I prefer that they learn how to collect qualitative data in a site that is new to them. It makes the process of learning how to see with ethnographic eyes easier and less complicated. It allows the students to think about how they want to position themselves at the site in an unfettered way. As Emily Tancredi-Brice Agbenyega details in the following chapter, where you sit or how you position yourself in a site matters. While at times insider knowledge can be useful, to enter into a site as a novice researcher with a predetermined positionality as a member of that social world strikes me as adding an unnecessary level of difficulty to the already challenging process of becoming a qualitative researcher.

In addition to deciding where to sit at a site, both metaphorically and in reality, you will have to determine how you want to explain what you are doing at the site. Well-intentioned individuals at your research site will ask, at times out of simple, polite curiosity, "What are you taking those notes for?" Followed by, "Oh, it's research, on what?" Remember, these individuals are well-meaning. They do not intend to cause an existential crisis by asking you to explain what you are doing when you really often have little idea yourself. The best thing to do here is to be brief, honest, and direct with your answer or explanation. There is no reason to launch into an explanation of the whole project, how you came to be interested in it, and why you are not really sure what your research question is yet. People who ask are often just being polite. They may have a passing interest in what you are doing but usually that is really about it. My advice is to give an answer that is no longer than three sentences that is easily understood by the general public.

For students enrolled in my course this is easy. They have the cover of the class. Almost everyone has had to do a project for a class. So students often say something like (drawing on Rob's project), "I have to do a project for a class. So I am studying how students use the library." For dissertation work or other research a similarly simple explanation is usually what people are looking for. They are usually happy with something like, "I am interested in how the College Counseling Office works and so I am observing here for a few weeks," or "I am doing a project on computer use in classrooms," or "I am interested in students' experiences in entry-level science courses." Sometimes people ask you for more detail, but usually they do not. If someone wants more detail I usually talk about why I am interested in a particular phenomenon. So when someone asked why I wanted to understand how college counseling offices worked, I would tell them, "Different schools have different resources and approaches to how they help students get into college. I am interested in those differences and am observing here at Jefferson and at a couple of other schools as well."

Sometimes key informants at the site, those people you have talked with repeatedly at the site and observed often, want to know what you are finding. This, too, is reasonable. These individuals have likely been useful to you in generating insights on the goings-on at the site. They have gotten to know you and perhaps you feel grateful to them. You have likely talked with them about what you have seen as you try to make sense of your data in relation to your research question. What do you say to them?

Again, my advice is the same: provide simple, honest, and easily understood information. Try to follow your questioner's lead. If they smilingly ask you as you are passing them while going down a busy hallway, "How is it going?," simply smile and say, "Great!" If they seek you out and ask to talk privately with you and then upon meeting say they are concerned about something, listen carefully to their concerns and try to address them in an honest and direct way. If you need time to think about their concerns, say so. If they ask you what you are thinking or finding, think even more carefully before you answer.

In working with the participants at your site it is wise to avoid the temptation to gossip, even if it could build rapport; is done in a friendly, fun way; and does not seem to be hurtful. It is wise to follow the saying, If you can't say something nice, don't say anything at all. Your goal is to remain a neutral interested observer. While most organizations, classrooms, or other groups of people have different factions, you do not want to be aligned with any of them. To be aligned with any faction by definition means you are distanced from another. While sometimes you may have a special interest in one faction and so deepening your ties with them will make sense, in general, it is wise to remain unattached and friendly to all.

Likewise, it is unwise (and unethical) to discuss your research casually in public. It is best to be very careful in sharing your emerging thoughts on what you are seeing with anyone from the site. At times, it can be helpful to confide in key informants, to test ideas or ask for advice. You might learn a great deal from asking a friendly informant at the site, "Why does Joe always arrive late in the morning?" or "What does it mean when X happens?" or "Can you tell me about Y process?" This is different from sharing your own insights as you look for meaningful data or engaging in idle gossip. You are not a normal participant at this site. You are a researcher. The rules are different for you now. Often what you say carries more weight and you will use what you learn differently than a normal participant at the site. It can also undermine your project if you are viewed as untrustworthy. While some may confide in you, others will avoid you because of these perceived alliances. While you may have learned some "juicy details" about folks at the site, it is usually wise to keep them to yourself. Sharing insider information gained through your data collection efforts with others almost always leads to trouble managing your role at the site and usually does not lead to further fruitful data collection. Sharing this information also undermines the trust of your participants at the site.

A NEW WAY OF SEEING:
DEVELOPING ETHNOGRAPHIC EYES

To see the world as an ethnographer is to see it through a different set of eyes. This new set of lenses allows you to see the meaning in the routine, normal everyday activities of the participants of your study. Your ethnographic gaze is developed by encouraging a deep curiosity about the world, or this particular corner of it, and a desire to reveal the meaning found in the everyday interactions that make up this social world. You reveal the meaning in the details of this world and the meaning they have for the participants of the site. You do this through field notes based on your participant observation at the site and through talking with people there, either in formal or informal interviews. This attention to detail and meaning allows you to shed light on a process, place, or people of interest.

Beginning to see in a different way—to develop these ethnographic eyes—is a critical early part of your ethnographic journey. As you travel farther along on your journey you begin to wonder: What does it all mean? How do I make sense of what I am seeing? And how do I begin to tell anyone else about it? All three student chapters address these questions as they recount their own struggles to articulate meaning in their initial mini-ethnographies for my course. I also address these questions explicitly in Chapter 5.

NOTES

The term "Ethnographic Eyes" is taken from the title of the book *Ethnographic Eyes* by Carolyn Frank (1999, Heineman Press).

1. Carolyn Frank, in her wonderful book *Ethnographic Eyes*, argues that teachers can benefit from developing an ethnographic perspective. This ethnographic perspective enables them to see the world from a more objective standpoint that makes the implicit norms of classroom life explicit.

2. These images were introduced to me by my friend and colleague Ellen Skilton-Sylvester when she was a guest speaker in my class.

3. The author of this field note only notes the race of the African American and Hispanic participants here. In an earlier note the author noted that at this predominantly White school it would be assumed in his notes that all participants would be described as White and that he would only then note race when the participant was not White. This is a time-saving strategy—to set one race or gender as a default and note only those participants who do not fit this pattern.

Erin Horvat

While some research projects are more complicated than others, all qualitative research is complicated by the notion of positionality. Specifically, all qualitative researchers must figure out how they will position themselves at the research site. As Emily Tancredi-Brice Agbenyega, a 4th-year doctoral student, explains in the following chapter, this positionality has many facets. In addition to exploring how one's own identity influences what one sees and calls data at the research site, a researcher's data collection and analysis procedures are also affected by role management issues as well as simply figuring out where best to literally position oneself physically at the site to collect data that will be relevant to their research questions. In the chapter that follows Emily addresses how understanding where to best position yourself at the site is both an iterative and crucial part of fieldwork.

Emily's project for my class built on prior work she had done on a funded project for me and another researcher. While this prior knowledge of the topic and familiarity with a key informant were useful in understanding issues at the site and establishing rapport, it presented other challenges as Emily tried to separate her own fieldwork from that of the larger project and maintain her role as a researcher with her key informant. Emily also reflects on the way in which her sociocultural identity affected her fieldwork. Her most substantive contribution, however, is her in-depth exploration of the way in which she learned how her physical and theoretical position at the site influenced her fieldwork—how where she sat both physically in the space and how she positioned her understanding of what she was seeing—shaped her project.

Unlike other forms of research, in most qualitative research the researcher is the instrument of data collection. That is, rather than using a survey or questionnaire to collect responses from respondents, the data that you collect in doing fieldwork, especially field notes, are filtered through the senses (usually the eyes and ears) of the researcher. As the instrument of data collection, the researcher needs to be aware of her positionality, both *who* she is and *where* she physically positions herself at the site, as well as how she manages relationships with participants at the site because these factors influence her fieldwork. Emily's narrative explores these issues and provides useful advice for beginning qualitative researchers.

It Matters Where You Sit

Reflecting on the Role of Positionality in Qualitative Research

Emily Tancredi-Brice Agbenyega

When I walked in for the first time to observe the introductory chemistry lecture, Dr. J signaled for me to come to where she stood at the front of the hall. She greeted me, smiled at my pregnant state, and suggested that I take a seat. She pulled out a chair that had been set up at the desk next to the podium and set it to her left, directly in front of the hall. She seemed to tacitly say that this would be a good place to sit where I could see the whole hall and thus do a thorough observation of her class.

Looking up into the lecture hall, I could see a sea of ethnically diverse faces looking down toward where I stood by Dr. J's podium. The class was scheduled to begin in several minutes. It was early spring, one of the first warm days, and there was a buzz of excitement in the air. Students were still filing in and there was the sound of lecture seat desks squeaking open, students zipping open their bags, and textbooks banging onto the desks. The lecture hall was steep and narrow and sat circa 200 students. Nearly every seat was filled.

I appreciated Dr. J's getting a seat for me and, 7 months pregnant with my second child, I was not about to refuse the opportunity to sit. I thanked her and asked if it would be all right with her if I sat toward the side of the front of the hall. She shrugged and said I could sit where I liked. I pulled the chair to the far side of the hall so that I was sitting against the wall, directly next to the front row of students. I could still see the whole lecture hall from a perspective similar to the professor's, yet didn't feel like I was totally "on display" sitting in the front of the hall for all to see.

This excerpt from my field notes describes my first attempt as a research assistant to observe the introductory chemistry class in which many of my interviewees were enrolled. Our research team had begun its first semester of a funded mixed-method project looking at the cognitive and motivational variables associated with students' persistence in Science Technology

Engineering and Math (STEM) majors. Our team had heard about this particular introductory chemistry course and its professor during the interviews and so wished to gain firsthand experience of the class. The introductory chemistry professor, who was also part of the research team, wanted to get an objective view of her teaching as well as an additional perspective of students' engagement in the lecture. The professors directing the team asked me, as the research assistant focusing on the qualitative portion of the mixed-method project, to observe her lecture and take note of the general atmosphere of the lecture hall, her teaching style, and students' apparent receptivity toward Dr. J's instruction.

Having done only a few observations prior to this project, I went in with every intention of being in a "tabula rasa" state so that I could absorb whatever was around me. I wanted to see as much as possible about each component of the classroom that I had been asked to observe. For example, what was the atmosphere of the lecture hall—was it tense, energized, or drowsy? What was Dr. J's approach to teaching—was it forced, natural, or characterized by other traits? And how did students receive Dr. J's teaching? Did they appear to like her teaching style? Because the research team wanted to get a "general sense" of the classroom, I needed to observe as many details as possible about as much of the classroom as possible.

At the same time, I didn't want to be seen. Instead, I naively wanted to be invisible and thus not "alter" the conditions of my site. Intellectually I knew this was difficult, if not impossible. I understood from my brief study of qualitative research paradigms that I, as the researcher, would shape my research to some extent (Hesse-Biber & Leavy, 2006; Willis, 2007). Initially I wanted to be just an observer from afar without disrupting the setting. By the end of the project, I learned that this was impossible: Like my shadow, my positionality followed me everywhere. The scenario described in my field notes above was an early sign that any hopes I had for doing research without the shadow of my positionality following me were not to be realized. Even in walking in and deciding where to sit, I found my positionality—specifically, where I was physically positioned at the site—as the first barrier to seeing all that I wanted to see. My positionality influenced how I saw the site, the questions I asked, and where I chose to position myself. This chapter traces the journey I took as I grappled with various aspects of my positionality in an effort to collect data that addressed an answerable research question.

A year later, I returned to observe Dr. J's class for my qualitative research project for Professor Horvat's class. I found that such moments of indecision surrounding where to sit, what to observe, and how to manage my positionality characterized my data collection process throughout. Briefly, the initial goal of my project for Professor Horvat's class was to explore the relationship between the instructional "message" (i.e., expectations for student learning, including both skills and values) of a particular intro-ductory chemistry professor (Dr. J) and her students' perceptions of that "message." From my work as a research assistant I had heard students' voices—literally, in interviews—regarding their experience in the course. What I hoped to learn more about in my class project was what the profes-sor appeared to be teaching and how that fit with what the students per-ceived themselves to be learning. I expected that I would learn more about this relationship through observing the lectures and the professor's office hours as well as through one-on-one interviews with both the professor and a handful of students. While my overarching goal remained constant—to sit in the "best" place where I could collect data that would enable me to produce knowledge that was useful in some way for the participants as well as for my small study—my relationship to my research was dynamic and fraught with periods of indecision about *where* this "best" place was. I continually grappled with my positionality.

CHAPTER OVERVIEW

The notion of "where to sit" provides a metaphor for the many methodolog-ical decisions I made throughout my project. From the start, I was engaged in a "sit-where-the-fit-is" quest in which I continually struggled to balance three aspects of my positionality: (1) Where I physically placed myself at the site to collect data to best answer, or fit, my research question; (2) how I managed my role as both a novice researcher in Professor Horvat's class and as a research assistant with prior experience working with Dr. J on a sepa-rate though related project; and (3) how my sociocultural identity shaped the questions I was asking about my site and the methods I chose to answer those questions. In my project, these aspects of my positionality combined to create a "sit-where-the-fit-is" cycle in which my positionality in fieldwork—where I sat in the lecture hall both physically and in terms of the questions I was asking—was the primary influence. Managing my roles and framing my identity relative to my research were secondary factors. Accordingly, the bulk of the chapter is devoted to addressing how I determined to position myself during fieldwork in order to answer my research questions. I take up issues of role management and identity briefly at the end of the chapter. In deconstructing the experience I had, I hope to reveal what I learned about the importance of positionality and its role in the research process, provide the novice researcher a glimpse of the positional journey that lies ahead, and sug-gest some strategies that you can use to manage your positionality effectively.

My thinking about positionality was pushed along by a reflexive process that Professor Horvat fostered in our course. Specifically, she asked us to submit weekly field notes including our observer comments (our reflections both during and following our observations), and biweekly memos, which were longer, more detailed reflections on our research process. Through my observer comments and memos, I was able to reflect on my data (i.e., my field notes) and then analyze it to find my role in shaping the data I had collected (i.e., what analytical choices I had made by choosing to sit in certain locations, both physically and theoretically, and what I did or did not observe as a result of where I sat, either by choice or by circumstance). True to Professor Horvat's suggestion in Chapter 5 that "writing is analysis," the iterative process of collecting data and reflecting on it allowed me to see that where I sat, my role as a researcher, shaped the questions I asked, the data I collected, and the conclusions I drew.

MANAGING POSITIONALITY IN FIELDWORK: THE "SIT-WHERE-THE-FIT-IS" CYCLE

The "sit-where-the-fit-is" cycle consisted of a continual methodological and theoretical quest for collecting data that addressed an answerable research question. Through an iterative, or back-and-forth, process of collecting data to answer my research question and reflecting on these data, both my data collection methods and my question evolved and thus enabled me to attain my desired goal: a well-defined, answerable research question derived from my interest and grounded in what I was seeing in the field. I started off my project wanting to better understand Dr. J's instructional intentions *and* the students' receipt of that instruction. As I observed Dr. J's lectures and other course-related sessions (e.g., office hours), I reflected on my findings and realized that my initial questions—such as what was Dr. J's overall instructional "message" and how did students receive that "message"—were unanswerable given the scope of the project (i.e., a semester-long course assignment) and the existing circumstances on the ground (i.e., what I was actually observing as opposed to what I expected/wanted to observe). As qualitative researchers Hesse-Biber and Leavy (2006) explain, the process of collecting data, reflecting on it in light of my positionality, revising my questions, and returning to the field combined to form an iterative process, what I termed a "sit-where-the-fit-is" cycle, that recurred throughout my research project.

First Forays Into the Field

For our first assignment, before we began our observations, Professor Horvat gave us the task of drafting a site prospectus that outlined the goals for our project and included a brief description of where we planned to

observe and the data collection methods we expected to employ. Looking
back to my site prospectus, I can see that I had unreasonably lofty goals for
my project from the start:

> During the lectures, I will focus on how the professor defines and presents the
> overall goals for the course and her expectations for students' success in the
> course. I expect that this will be articulated through her class management,
> her explanation of concepts and her review of material in preparation for
> exams. How does she communicate her "message" regarding course goals
> and students' success in the course (defined as attaining the course goals)?
> To what extent does she translate her beliefs into practice? And, to foster a
> dialogical, interpretivist lens, what are the students experiencing and how
> does this fit with the professor's intentions and practice?

I saw potential questions everywhere! I didn't want to miss anything
and so erred on the side of asking numerous, broad questions. I wanted to
understand the professor's intentions and actions fully and so knew that I
needed to ask about what she taught, how she taught it, and what she believed about her subject matter and teaching techniques. I also believed that
to gain a deeper understanding of the professor's instructional intentions,
I needed to hear directly from the students about whether those intentions
were actually achieved. As a result, for my first few observations, I went into
the lecture hall and tried to observe *everything* about how the professor was
teaching: what she was wearing, her tone, her mannerisms/gesticulations,
words she frequently used, how and when she called on students, which
students she called on and how she responded, as well as how students
seemed to be reacting to her instruction. As Professor Horvat explained in
Chapter 3, I was in "vacuum" mode. I wanted to see anything that had to
do with the professor's articulation of course goals and criteria for students'
success and so recorded in my field notes that I wrote up during the lectures
and filled out following my observations as many related details as possible.
Here is an excerpt from my first set of field notes to illustrate my effort to
"vacuum up" as much data as I could:

> Both students next to me and those around me that I could see were
> copying down the outline. [Dr. J] narrated as she wrote. She was standing
> at the podium, using a black ink pen to write the outline on white, lined
> paper which was projected onto the screen behind her. She was wearing a
> grey sweater and a knee-length black skirt. I don't recall seeing her shoes.
> Her hair was grey and fell below her chin. She wore round-framed, silver-
> rimmed glasses and a thin headband or barrette (couldn't tell) that held
> her hair back from her face except part of the left side that framed her face.

I think she was wearing a necklace. She has pointy facial features. I don't remember her eye color, though I have been able to see her eyes closely during conversation.

I felt like I had to type very fast to get her outline all down. She said: "So, finish up. If you can't read it, ask your neighbor. Questions? So go ahead! Do your consultation, do it quickly." She waited 5 to 10 seconds and then said, "Who's ready to go on? Ask your question! So, come on, let's ask your questions," then we can be sure and then we can move on. Her tone felt simultaneously harsh and supportive—in the sense of wanting to clarify. *I wondered, How do students perceive her tone? Do they feel able to ask questions?*

Here, I was trying to see everything about the professor and capture at least some details relevant to the students. Sitting in the rear of lecture hall, I thought I would be able to see as many students as possible as well as the professor, who tended to circulate throughout the hall as she lectured. The appearance of the professor, what she said, how she said it, and how students reacted were all within the justifiable scope of my observations.

Typically, despite my best intentions, I found myself rushing at the last minute to my research site—the chem lecture. I would arrive out of breath just before class started and grab a seat in the back, happy not to have missed the start of class. Since I often entered the lecture hall just as class was starting, I usually sat either in one of few available seats in the back or, when no seats were available, at the top of the steps in the hall where I actually couldn't see the professor that well and definitely didn't see many students—other than the backs of their heads! Because at this point I just wanted to gather general information about Dr. J's instructional "message," and students' receipt of that message, my parameters for where it was best to sit were likewise broad. As a result, I was collecting a wide breadth of data without much depth. With what I had after my first few observations, I could say *a little* about *a lot* that was happening in the class. With my less than ideal last-minute seat-finding pattern, I was cataloguing a lot of detailed information but I didn't know what was important or why seemingly significant details even appeared significant. What could I say a little about? For instance, in regards to any message the professor conveyed, I could say that she had a tone that often reflected sarcasm and phrases that, at times, reflected encouragement. I couldn't say when her tone sounded sarcastic (i.e., in response to students' questions? At the end of class?) or at what points during the class she tended to speak words of encouragement. I hadn't focused solely on Dr. J's classroom speech and so didn't have enough data to notice trends regarding her speech. Regarding students' receipt of her "message," I could say almost nothing, as I always sat behind all of them! For each of my initial questions, I had collected some data yet I didn't have any even seemingly solid pattern that I was following. Like a vacuum, I had collected bits and pieces of data off of the broad surface of my site.

Reflection Through Memos

After our first couple of weeks in the field, Professor Horvat assigned us the task of writing a "memo" on our experience up to that point. For the first memo assignment, we were asked to reflect on the data we had collected and how it had felt being in the field. We were supposed to write three to five pages on our general thoughts about our site, particular challenges we'd faced and any initial patterns we'd found in our data. When I reviewed my notes, it became clear to me that I was trying to see too much about too many aspects of the class. I began my memo as follows:

> I find it a challenge to focus on my research question, which has three parts that I see as interrelated: How does she communicate her "message" regarding course goals and students' success in the course (defined as attaining the course goals)? To what extent does she translate her beliefs into practice? . . . What are the students experiencing and how does this fit with the professor's intentions and practice? After spending a couple weeks observing, I think I need to hone my focus and look at the following questions: What are the main skills and attitudes the professor expects/desires the students to take away from the course? What are the main skills and attitudes students think the professor expects them to learn? And, finally, what are the main skills and attitudes they think they *actually* take away? Based on what I've seen so far, I think my original questions are too loaded, based too much on my own limited view that the professor has a "message" she's trying to get across.

Through my memo assignment, I was able to understand how where I sat in the hall influenced what data I was able to gather, what I was literally able to see, and also how my research questions affected my data collection. Literally, because I frequently sat in the back of the lecture hall, I learned about what Dr. J's tone felt like primarily from afar. I didn't know if or how the atmosphere of the hall felt different from the middle or front of the room. I literally had a limited perspective of both Dr. J and the students.

I also realized that my perspective was limited figuratively as well by the questions I was asking. For example, by asking a question about the "message" Dr. J conveyed through her instruction, I was poised to focus on Dr. J's tone and speech content and perhaps be blinded to other aspects of her instruction or even inconsistencies in her statements that might indicate she didn't have a uniform "message" she was passing on to her students. My questions allowed me to see some details and blinded me to others.

Even from my first sets of field notes, I could see that I wasn't going to be able to directly observe Dr. J's "message," as I vaguely defined it; instead, I could see patterns in her tone and in what she said to her students during lectures. I could see the clear expression of Dr. J's expectations and her tone that at times matched these expectations and at other times negated them. In particular, my "observer comments," the brief reflections in brackets—[]'s—or *italics* I wrote either as I took notes in the field or when I was writing up my field notes afterward, revealed further questions I had about what I was observing as well as budding patterns in the data. During my 1st week of observations, I noted:

> She continued reading the case study introduction posted on Blackboard. It was a Word document which she read verbatim. [I noted that students have all these directions in writing.] In the document, there was a sentence that said that case studies would be introduced Monday, January 25, 2010 with PowerPoint slides and a video. [Wow, everything seems so pre-planned/organized. How does this enable clear expectations and realization of those expectations? Does this enable authentic learning? How will I/we define authentic learning?].
>
> Dr. J explained that students would grade each other. She said, you are responsible for evaluating, grading five other people—just your group, because I can't possibly be writing everything down and facilitating, so I will trust that you can do that [this seemed to be a mix of encouraging and mildly stern/sarcastic—is this solely her tone or her actual attitude?]

My observer comments are in brackets here. This observation regarding Dr. J's expectations and the tone of her voice throughout the lecture was confirmed in subsequent observations. I saw that Dr. J would ask students questions that conveyed, though perhaps indirectly, her expectations for what students should know as beginning chemists. In the memo I referenced earlier, I went on to posit:

> Regarding Dr. J's effort to involve students in the class, I have been struck by how many questions she asks throughout the lecture and how she asks various students to respond. Although I have yet to start a chart to count how many questions she asks in each lecture, on average, and what types of questions she asks (i.e., ranging from basic information recall to higher-order analysis), it seems that there are at least ten questions per lecture. The questions she asks range from requests for fact recall to asking if students had seen or experienced something related to the lecture topic. Her

questions sometimes can be answered with information she has just taught and other times require responses with deeper conceptual understanding or connections with material covered in prior lectures. Sometimes she seems to just check in to make sure students are following her. I only observed her asking one or two questions that were intentionally rhetorical.

I had recorded Dr. J's questions either verbatim or in paraphrased form in an effort to see "everything"—or at least as much as I could possibly see regarding this aspect of her instruction and how it may have conveyed her expectations for students' success in the course. Most of my observer comments revealed that I *was* noticing patterns regarding Dr. J's instruction; however, they were patterns surrounding not her "message," but her instructional tactics: namely, the frequency with which she asked questions and tried to encourage active class participation in a lecture setting.

In one of my memos, I had begun to make sense of the bits and pieces of data I had collected while in "vacuum" mode. Although where I sat and the questions I was asking combined to give me a limited perspective on my site, I was at least able to collect data that revealed the frequency of Dr. J's questioning and possible patterns in the types of questions she asked. The data I collected showed me that Dr. J did in fact have instructional habits (e.g., question-asking and outline-creation) and that perhaps these were worth focusing on. My vacuum mode, though difficult, was thus not as futile as it first seemed; rather, it was a necessary first step so that I could then reflect and begin to sort out what I had learned.

In my memo exercise, I drew from my field notes, including my observer comments, the highlights of my observations. I was able to take stock of what I was seeing from where I sat thus far and to reflect on whether I needed to tweak my questions or sit in a different place at my site to better answer my question. The answer was both. And so the "sit-where-the-fit-is" cycle began: having reflected on my data, I realized that I needed to sit in a different place to better answer my now refined research questions. My notions of "message" were not rooted, at least yet, in the reality I was seeing; thus, I needed to ask more concrete questions about the skills and attitudes (i.e., approaches to learning chemistry) Dr. J wanted her students to learn and I therefore needed to sit in a place that would enable me to collect data that would effectively address these questions. Rushing in to find an available seat in the back would not allow me to find the "best" seat; so I intentionally needed to choose seats in the lecture hall that would help me learn more about Dr. J's communication of the skills and attitudes that students needed to succeed in her class.

Before outlining my next cycle of seat-finding, I think it is important to note briefly that this initial stage of not knowing where best to sit is a necessary one. As Bradley Bergey (Chapter 6) notes in his exploration of what he calls the second of three stages of blindness one faces as one tries to find the ideal research question, the experience of seeing potential research questions everywhere is a necessary step along the research journey. Such bumbling about, as Professor Horvat noted, can be frustrating; however, it's necessary afterward to ask an even more refined research question that more aptly fits your data and then proceed to position yourself at your research site in a place where you can effectively collect data to answer that question. And then the cycle continues, for there is nothing tidy about qualitative research.

Returning to the Field

So, having memoed and now armed with new and, I hoped, improved research questions, I returned to the field. As my questions were now more focused, I needed to sit more intentionally at my site rather than just grabbing a convenient seat. My next step was to experiment with this intentional sitting exercise and, yes, you guessed it, reflect again on whether I was "sitting where the fit was." As a reminder, my revised questions were:

What are the main skills and attitudes the professor expects/desires the students to take away from the course? What are the main skills and attitudes students think the professor expects them to learn? And, finally, what are the main skills and attitudes they think they *actually* take away?

During the 3rd week of data collection, I realized that Dr. J's questioning technique was her predominant mode of instruction and so likely a useful focal point for learning about her expectations for skills and attitudes students needed to succeed in her course. Accordingly, I initiated a new data collection technique aimed at gathering data relevant to my new focal point: Dr. J's questions. In a reflection in my second set of field notes, which included observations from weeks 2 and 3 of the total 7 weeks of the project, I noted: "Reflection: The Questions are frequent. She also does explicitly state her expectations during the course of the lecture. How can I focus on this? General thoughts: I think starting tomorrow (Friday) I need to have a chart for questions—their type, frequency, and students' responses, including demographics of the students who respond." The chart thus allowed me to hone my focus—to transition from vacuum to spotlight mode. In my charting, I tracked the questions by type, the students' response to each question, the responders' demographics (i.e., gender, race/ethnicity if determinable), and any response Dr. J made to the responders. With the chart I was able to see, and hear, verbatim, what types of questions Dr. J asked, how she asked them, to whom she directed them, who responded, and how Dr. J fielded the response. The chart itself was a vantage point from which I could see in a more nuanced way what skills and attitudes Dr. J expected her students to acquire. As a result of focusing my observations, of trying to sit where the fit was, I was able to *see* more, specifically more details that were relevant to my research question. For instance, I noted the following:

> How does Dr. J choose who she calls on to answer questions, especially if no student raises his/her hand? To what extent does she purposefully diversify the student participation? I found the charting useful for seeing patterns, though I found it might have narrowed my focus too much—or not if I really do just want to focus on questions? It was interesting to be able to notice a pattern in types of questions just by creating a chart. I'll continue to use the chart but need to figure out which information to keep track of. I realized that it's difficult to capture the whole "communication moment": Dr. J's question, students' response, then Dr. J's follow-up, though at least I do see this pattern. I'll need to get at this in the interviews: What is Dr. J's intention with her questions? How do students experience these questions? What skills/attitudes does Dr. J hope to cultivate through these questions? And what skills/attitudes do students take away from these questions? Compared to other aspects of the lecture (i.e., clicker questions, Dr. J's monologuing, etc.)? It is nice to be able to focus on just one aspect of Dr. J's instruction and see what fruit it bears!

Here, I was able to notice patterns because of my increased focus on one particular aspect of Dr. J's instruction. Although I found the charting method unwieldy at first—that is, "difficult to capture the whole 'communication moment'"—the benefits of such focus exceeded the challenges. You can see, in fact, that I referenced my new research questions specifically. I was able to ask these more refined questions not only about Dr. J but about the students as well.

After several observations using the charts, I saw that a pattern arose not only in the types of questions Dr. J asked, but in who responded. In one particular observation, I purposefully focused on the students and sat accordingly. At the start of each of my field notes, I briefly summarized what the focal point of my observation had been and the highlights from my observation. In my observation focused on the students, I noted the following:

What I was looking for:

> I was still looking for patterns in Dr. J's communication of expectations, skills, and attitudes, specifically through her questioning and explicitly stated

expectations. I also was hoping to really focus on the students and identify who was responding to the questions. I needed to sit in the front and arrive on time—and I did!

What stood out and why:

The same white male students *do* respond to Dr. J's questions. She also called on a white male student whom she had called on before. At the same time though there were a number of female students of color who responded. Specifically, 6 different white male students responded, 1 Asian male, 1 Black female, circa 2 white females, and 1 Indian male student responded. This seems like an uneven distribution, especially given that the class is more than half students of color and more than 60% female. It would be great to interview a diverse group of students—in terms of ethnicity, gender, and performance, to see how their experience of the class varies.

While issues of student diversity were in the back of my mind even prior to the start of this particular project, they were not the focus of this research project; however, because of where I sat, how I collected data and what I chose to pay attention to, I collected data that revealed the significant role that student diversity played at my site and saw how it might relate to my research question. Perhaps the issue of diversity didn't relate directly to the skills and attitudes students thought they were expected to acquire or those skills and attitudes they actually did acquire, but it certainly related to *which* students were likely acquiring any skills or attitudes to a greater extent than others due to the question-asking pattern of Dr. J.

In my second memo assignment, I pondered the role that diversity might play at my site:

There is definitely a disproportionate number of white male students who respond to and are called on to respond to questions. Overall, they seem to respond with confidence. The male students of color also seemed to respond with confidence, yet they were fewer in number. At least two of the female students who responded seemed confident in their answers, while a few seemed a bit hesitant. Overall, of the students who were called upon—who didn't have their hands raised—male students seemed more confident in their answers than female students. I will need to keep observing for student responses to see any kind of even temporary trend; however, the potential patterns thus far are interesting. Are male students less phased by Dr. J's demeanor? Due perhaps to their prior schooling? Dr. J had mentioned that female students had been shown to perform slightly better in her course than Dr. H's, the male professor's course—how does this play out in the actual lectures? Are there a higher number of female students who respond to her questions? If so, are these voluntarily participating students or those Dr. J calls on? I'll need to focus my remaining lecture observations on this.

Again, with the reflective space of the memo, I was able to canvas my data—charts, in this case—and see that a couple of key patterns had appeared. First, patterns existed in the types of questions Dr. J asked and a student-response pattern defined by race and gender had emerged, even if only tentatively. Where I sat enabled me to focus on the reality-on-the ground, the actual circumstances at my site, rather than my vague, presumed notions about Dr. J's "message" or even my tentative thoughts regarding the likely mismatch between what Dr. J thought she was teaching and what students felt they were learning in the course. Interestingly, my prior research and personal experience had taught me to expect the raced, gendered patterns of class participation I observed; where I sat here at my site during this qualitative research project enabled me to collect data that, dishearteningly, confirmed my hunches and led me to ask more pointed questions about frequency of class participation (as defined by question-asking), the root causes of the patterns, and the distinctions between voluntary and instructor-led class participation.

Final Forays into the Field

It would seem as a result of this refinement that shifting my focus to the students would have been the next natural phase of my sit-where-the-fit is cycle for, as a result of my memos, I was able to see what I *wasn't* seeing in my observations: direct perspectives from students. Although I had hoped to ascertain students' perspectives, I found that in the course of 7 weeks, I could barely gain a nuanced understanding of the professor's expectations, much less the students', too. Although I had gone through the sit-where-the-fit-is cycle twice and was now armed with more focused research questions that got at specific details related to the students, I was in the final couple of weeks of data collection for the class project and needed to turn my focus to data analysis. I found myself torn between collecting more data on the professor's instructional tactics so that I could begin to approach a saturation point regarding her questioning patterns and trying to collect meaningful data on students' learning. At this point in my journey, I realized that while trying to learn more about what I wasn't seeing clearly (i.e., the students and their perspectives) would be interesting and would address my latest set of revised questions, I instead needed to zoom in with my spotlight on the professor and save my questions regarding the students for later.

Collecting additional data on Dr. J's instruction would allow me to have enough evidence to support the emergent patterns in my data. I would have more data on her questioning tactics directed toward "thinking like a chemist," those involving classroom management, and others apparently aimed at encouraging class participation. In the spirit of Professor Horvat's "more is more" description regarding data collection, I strove, as a novice qualitative researcher, for a deeper understanding of a slice of the reality I observed.

My urgency about developing a focus was due in large part to the stringent and arbitrary guidelines for the project: 1 to 2 weeks to confirm a site, 6 to 7 weeks to collect data (depending on when the site was confirmed), spending 3 to 4 hours per week in the field, and the remaining 4 weeks to analyze it and write up a final report; however, *all* projects have boundaries. Even for a longer project such as a dissertation, data collection cannot be unending. In the case of sponsored research, reports have deadlines as well, and funding runs out. While many iterations between revised research questions and repeated forays into the field can continue to produce increasingly nuanced understandings of our research site/topic, the boundaries of any given project require even the most expert researcher to force her focus and intentionally limit her data collection at some point (Lareau & Shultz, 1996).

Having memoed a third and final time, and with my focus set, I continued in my sit-where-the-fit-is cycle and began my last round of data collection with the aim of answering only my first research question: What are the main skills and attitudes the professor expects/desires the students to take away from the course? I continued to sit where I could chart more questions and see different groups of students' responses. I sat in the front, sides, rear, and middle of the lecture hall, because I could observe and document different levels of engagement in each section. Sitting in these different spaces allowed me to experience the class, to a limited extent, as a student might. Although the student perspective was no longer my focus, I grew in my understanding of Dr. J's instructional tactics by sitting in various student-eye-view positions.

During these last couple of weeks of data collection, I also chose to observe spaces outside of the lecture hall that would give me yet another perspective on Dr. J's instruction. From the start of the project I had hoped to observe Dr. J's office hours. At this point I knew that observing her office hours would still help me to answer my first research question and so decided to keep this aspect of my research design. I also chose to observe several small-group case-study sessions that were a part of the course so I could see Dr. J in a different instructional setting. Observing both the office-hour and case-study sessions gave me a deeper understanding of Dr. J's questioning-asking and the diversity patterns I had observed in the lecture and helped me to learn about her instruction overall.

The office-hour session I observed shed a different light on the question-asking and diversity patterns. In Dr. J's interactions with several of her students one-on-one, I could see how she asked students many questions, other than classroom management questions, even in this setting. I was also able to learn more about the several students who came: their class year, their goals for the course, their prior school experience that had—or hadn't—prepared them for this course, and what they were learning or struggling to learn. Dr. J clearly wanted to know about each individual student's' background related to the course (e.g., What other science courses had they taken in high school? How did they study in high school? How did they study differently for this course?). Her curiosity about each student helped me to ask more questions about diversity patterns I noticed: Was Dr. J conscious of the raced or gendered patterns of question-answering in her class? In her one-on-one interactions with students, she seemed equally inquisitive of all of them and, in this way, didn't appear to discriminate based on the individual background of the student.

My case-study observations also deepened my understanding of and added to my questions about the diversity patterns I had observed in the lecture. Having learned that this was one of few graded assignments in addition to the lecture exams, as well as one of the only additional spaces where professor-led instruction took place outside the lecture hall, I felt it important to observe several sessions. Because I did these observations primarily during "Round 3" of data collection, I was able to implement my charted, more focused method of observing. In the beginning summary of my field notes, I noted the following:

What stood out and why:

It was somewhat disheartening to see my expectations fulfilled: when guessing who would act as spokespeople for the groups, I saw that, indeed, the white male students were the initial spokespeople, although the female post-bac students spoke up later.

Reflection

Like in the lectures, I am seeing the race/gender piece play a role in who participates obviously . . . in both the case study and lecture sessions. WM [white male] students just seem more comfortable speaking in class. To what extent do Dr. H and Dr. J, neither of whom are WM's, see this? Perhaps race/gender are key pieces to look for in remaining observations and to ask about in interviews?

By sitting intentionally in this different space, yet armed with the same research questions, I was able to supplement and confirm my other data collected primarily from lecture observations. As many qualitative researchers explain, I was in this way able to triangulate my data: I could take my data from the lecture observations, identify patterns, and then look at other instructional spaces to either confirm or disconfirm those patterns (e.g., Hesse-Biber & Leavy, 2006). In the case-study session, I saw a similar trend in classroom participation occurring predominantly among the white male students regardless of whether students volunteered to speak or the professor engaged students directly.

The Final Write-Up

The semester drawing quickly to a close, our final chance for analysis arrived after 7 weeks of being in the field: the draft of our final ethnographic report that needed to be a story, to have a beginning, middle, and end. Being at the close of another sit-where-the-fit-is cycle with the realization that I couldn't go back into the field with even better questions and sit in an even more effective place to answer those questions or collect different forms of data such as interviews and begin the cycle once again felt frustrating. The perfectionist and continuously curious parts of me thirsted for another chance, for more concrete answers, for more data!

My final review of my observation and interview data revealed that the overarching theme of Dr. J's instructional tactics and students' perceptions was that to learn chemistry and to be a chemist were difficult feats to accomplish. To be successful in the course was thought by all—including Dr. J!—to be a near-impossible task. The skills and attitudes that Dr. J expected students to have or to develop all centered around the challenge of mastering the difficulty of Dr. J's exams as well as the field of chemistry as a whole. Dr. J was trying to teach successfully and the students were trying to learn effectively; however, as evidenced by exam averages of 45%, neither of these efforts was successful. There was a gap between what Dr. J was teaching and what students were actually learning. Additionally, the diversity patterns likely had implications for students' attempts to succeed in the course. Despite Dr. J's equitable one-on-one treatment in settings such as her office hours, the patterns observed in the lectures and small-group case-study sessions showed that not all students were participating in the course at the same levels. This led to the question of *why* this was the case.

While my findings were tentative at best, they were rooted primarily in the observational data I had collected and displayed my current understanding of Dr. J's instruction at that point in time. While collecting more data would have allowed me to explore these emergent patterns further, all projects have boundaries and I had reached mine. The report was due and I needed to say what I could about the data I actually had. Recall the initial "vacuum" mode I was in when I started my project, where I noted how I could say a *little* about a *lot* in the course? At the end point of my project, having been in "spotlight" mode for several weeks, I felt that I could at least say *something significant* about a *little* in the course. Through several "sit-where-the-fit-is" cycles, I had managed to transition from "vacuum" to "spotlight" mode and collect data that effectively addressed a single, answerable research question: What are the main skills and attitudes the professor expects/desires the students to take away from the course?

THE LONG SHADOW CAST BY POSITIONALITY: ROLE MANAGEMENT AND SOCIAL IDENTITY

Recall the "shadow" I mentioned at the start of this chapter. My positionality, like a shadow, followed me everywhere. While the quandary of where to sit in the lecture hall reflected the most obvious features of my shadow and its impact on my research, the other aspects of my positionality were likewise important in my fieldwork. Both the multiple roles I had at the research site and my own social identity influenced my research.

Role Management: Wearing Multiple Hats

The feeling of wearing multiple hats characterized my struggle to manage my role in the midst of my sit-where-the-fit-is cycles in two major ways: (1) with regard to my research focus and questions; and (2) in terms of building rapport with my key informant, Dr. J. While the "hats" I wore might be unique to me, the notion of role management is innate to any qualitative research project. You will always need to manage your role in your research, whether due to prior experience at your site or because you develop complex relationships with participants over time. Before outlining the feeling of "wearing multiple hats," I will offer a bit of background about my particular circumstances.

As I noted in the introduction to this chapter, prior to starting the project for Professor Horvat's course, I had been part of a research team with Dr. J for over a year. I had sat in team meetings with her and thus heard her concerns regarding her course and her struggles to configure the course to better meet students' learning needs, especially in light of the fact that a high percentage of students failed the course each semester. As the graduate assistant in charge of organizing and carrying out the bulk of qualitative research on the project, I had interviewed approximately 20 chemistry students in her course by the time I started the qualitative data collection class and, as a result, saw the course through the lens of their experience. I had done initial observations such as the one cited at the start of the chapter and had developed rapport with Dr. J.

So even from the start of the project for Professor Horvat's course, I knew that my research focus would be shaped by my experience on the grant-funded project and would present the challenge of managing the multiple hats I wore in relation to my research questions and key informant, Dr. J. I knew I would need to distinguish between the research questions I had chosen to focus on for Professor Horvat's course and those broader research questions that were the focus of the grant-funded project on which I'd worked as a research assistant. While the grant-funded project goals overlapped with my course project research interests—we were looking at factors associated with student persistence in STEM majors— they were rooted in understanding the students' experience. As I explained in the chapter overview, this focus on the students' experience was a way into my project and in fact sparked my interest in learning more about Dr. J and her instruction. However, the students' experience was not the focal point of my own project for Professor Horvat's class. As a result, I had to distinguish between the questions being asked for the grant-funded project and the smaller-scale questions I was asking for my course project. Throughout my course project I could see how my desire to see "everything" was fueled in part by the broader focus of the grant-funded project. I thus periodically needed to acknowledge this desire to see "everything" and then consciously, though temporarily, blind myself to the goals of the larger project.

My struggles with role management also shaped the questions I felt were important to ask as a result of trying to maintain my rapport with Dr. J. Dr. J was deeply interested in learning about the impact of the case study assignment she had designed. She felt it reflected active, hands-on learning that could engage more students and thus offer them a path into succeeding in her notoriously difficult chemistry course. Knowing her interest in this particular assignment, I purposefully focused on it in my observations. I also knew that I needed to focus on the case-study assignment in relation to the other aspects of the course if I wanted to understand Dr. J's instructional methods comprehensively. I appreciated her desire to learn about this particular aspect of the course and wanted to incorporate her need to understand it more deeply into my research design; however, I needed to balance this with my own role and goals. As a result, while I observed several case-study sessions, I did not focus on them to the extent that Dr. J might have wished me to.

Perhaps every novice researcher will not have these specific roles to juggle; however, all qualitative researchers have connections to the world outside their research site and so will inevitably need to foster a balance between their own research interests and those of their informants which may, at times, conflict. Committing to this balance and staying in the space of ambiguity for at least some time will enable any novice researcher to wear many hats and still successfully complete their project.

Framing My Research: My Sociocultural Identity

In addition to the challenge of role management, my various social positions also "shadowed" my fieldwork. As a mother, my life circumstances played a role as far as balancing my family, work, and school commitments with my project-related tasks. My worldview, too, as a graduate student of color studying urban education, shaped how I viewed the social dynamics at my site. In my particular case, I had to tease out how each of these social positions and their related biases may have played a role in shaping the questions I was asking, how I was seeking to answer them, and how I analyzed the data I collected.

To start, being a mother with two young children initially shaped my interactions with Dr. J and set parameters for what I could realistically achieve within the scope of a semester-long project. My conversations with Dr. J always began with her asking "How are the kids?" and a funny anecdote would often be shared. She had a grandchild of a similar age as my elder daughter (about 5 years old, at the time), so we connected on the basis of delighting in kindergarten-age antics. While this was very useful for establishing rapport, I often felt that I then had to redefine myself as a student doing an independent research project in addition to being a mother.

Additionally, my time to write up field notes was extremely limited, so I found myself struggling with the need to be very disciplined and complete them in a timely manner. I learned the hard way that it is important not to collect more data before you have sufficiently processed what you have already collected (i.e., written up and reflected on field notes), otherwise you risk missing budding trends and seeing where your data is leading you (Lareau & Shultz, 1996). Due to family commitments, I often had to write in recollection more than 48 hours after the observation and thus reconstruct my observations. Both of these points related to being a mom are not unique to that particular situation: you surely have commitments that require your time and energy more urgently than your fieldwork as well; however, completing a high-quality project in the span of only a semester necessitates both solid time-management skills and a good dose of pragmatism. If you can't fully process all of your data, perhaps you can collect less data? While more is more, this is not the case if you are not fully able to analyze all you have seen.

My social position as a female graduate student of color studying urban education most strongly shaped my perceptions of student voice and equity in the course. While the issue of diversity came up quite naturally in my data as I started cataloguing class participation, it is likely that this took on more significance as a result of my worldview. The majority of my prior course-work touched on issues of diversity and (in)equity at elementary, secondary, and higher education levels of education. As a result, I felt attuned to seeing these issues in the world around me. Being a female student of color, my life experience had also given me a specific view of the world. I often see color, class, and gender inequities in my surroundings. Seeing this at my site thus seemed normal.

Through the reflective methods of writing observer comments as I took notes in the field and memoing periodically during the project, I was able to take time to think about how my multiple roles and various social positions shaped my research project. While the characteristics I noted may be pecu-liar to my situation, it is the case in any research project that the researcher's prior experience and personal circumstances will impact his or her research.

CONCLUSION

In addition to endeavoring both methodologically and theoretically to ask an answerable research question and sit in spaces that answered that ques-tion, I struggled to account for the roles I played in my research and the ways in which my sociocultural identity may have shaped my project and its outcomes. In many qualitative research paradigms, it is often the assump-tion that each aspect of our research process, which includes our research questions, our data collection techniques, and our methods of analysis, are shaped by *who* we are (Guba & Lincoln, 1994). That is, the roles that we occupy vis-à-vis our informants (e.g., equal social positions vs. hierarchical, just met vs. prior professional/friendship connection) and our social posi-tions more generally (e.g., our race, socioeconomic status, gender, education level, etc.) frame our research. While our positionality is unique to each of us as novice researchers—and surely even as we become more "expert"—the phenomenon of trying to account for our positionality as we journey through our research is likely universal.

As is explored in detail in *Journeys Through Ethnography*, a popular account of several well-known qualitative researchers' personal experi-ences with doing ethnography (i.e., qualitative research), every qualitative researcher is faced with challenges that may shape her effort to immerse herself in the iterative process of data collection and analysis (Lareau & Shultz, 1996). Viewed another way, this "shadow" in fact enriches the process of data collection and can, if accounted for fully, deepen our understanding of what we are seeing in the field. Real life as a researcher involves just that: real life.

It is my hope that this account of my experience will shed light on the iterative journey that qualitative research entails. This journey is for the most part cyclical: forays into the field followed by reflection on the effectiveness of one's methods in collecting data that address an answerable research question and then additional forays into the field with questions and methods revised according to the reflection. Our positionality is a shadow that follows us throughout this journey, at times disrupting the cycle as we try to manage our roles at our site and at other times giving us a keener vision into our data as a result of the social positions we occupy. Both the cycle and our shadow reinforce a most significant aspect of our journeys as novice qualitative researchers: it matters where you sit.

Part III

ANALYSIS AND WRITING

CHAPTER FIVE

Making Sense of What You Are Seeing

Analysis and Writing

Erin Horvat

It usually begins after students have been in the field for about 4 to 5 weeks. They have gained access to their site, managed to turn in one (or maybe two) set(s) of decent field notes, and pick their heads up long enough to realize that they have only a few weeks left in the class during which they will be collecting data. The due date for the first rough draft of their report suddenly looms. They come to class visibly pale as they report, with a mix of shock and whispered fear, "I don't have anything to say. I am seeing a lot of interesting things but I do not know what it means." In other words, they have no idea how they are going to answer their research question. This is especially hard for students who were sure they would be able to "show something." Those students who desperately wanted to unlock an important mystery (the causes of the achievement gap, why so many teachers leave the profession early in their careers, etc.) are especially angst-ridden at this point in the course. Like an explorer who has reached uncharted new lands, students at this juncture often do not know where to turn. How do they look at their data in a way that will help them tell an interesting story or answer a research question? Where do the diamonds lie in what they have collected and how do they find them? What do they *do* to get from piles of field notes and interview transcripts to a report or paper?

The answers usually lie in a researcher's original interest and curiosity. Why did you pick this site? What are you hoping to learn? Do you see anything that helps you understand this process, place, or people any better? Have you seen anything that you find compelling, even if you cannot articulate why you find it compelling? In addition to these types of questions, there are some techniques, tools, and practices that you can use to make sense of what you are seeing.

THE ANALYTIC TOOLKIT

In the same way that collecting qualitative data requires you to learn specific techniques and skills, the process of making sense of what you are seeing can be aided by engaging in specific analytic strategies. While there are times when it will have been clear from the moment you set foot at the site why specific actions are critical or meaningful, often we only have a vague idea that some particular exchange or interaction is important. It is often not until we use tools such as coding, writing, and talking to colleagues about our nascent insights in the field that we more fully understand and can articulate the meaning of what we are seeing. These tools allow us to bring our ideas, hunches, and insights from literature into conversation with the data yielding relevant findings. While most of the tools I describe in the section below are discrete activities researchers can do with their data, the first and really the most important tool is an understanding that data analysis is an ongoing process that is not confined to the post-data collection period.

Analysis Is an Ongoing Process, Not an Event

The process of making meaning or revealing the meaning of the actions at the site is something that happens during data collection and the ongoing emergent analysis engaged in by the researcher throughout the project. This analysis starts when you first pick a site or a topic of interest for your study. This initial naming and choosing of a topic and site is an analytic choice. By picking a site the researcher is by definition signaling that he thinks something interesting will be happening there. There is an analytic reason why the site has been selected. The analytic lens becomes more prominent when the researcher shifts from the vacuum cleaner style of field notes, where you are collecting everything you see, to the spotlight style, where you focus on and highlight specific interactions, processes, or events. In both instances the researcher is making analytic decisions about what to look at, where they think they will find it, and, in some ways, what it all means. Perhaps an example will help. I use the example of one of my students, Susan, below to illustrate how the analytic focus of a project develops over time as the researcher continually brings her interest and questions into conversation with the site and the data she is collecting over the life of the study.

Susan, a student in our literacy and language doctoral program, contacted me a few weeks before the course began. She was interested in reader identity and wanted to conduct her project at a site where she could investigate reader identity. She wanted to find a site where she could follow students through their day and observe how their reader identity changed in different classes/contexts. She had spent a good bit of time thinking about reader identity and so her learning agenda was pretty fully developed. She had a well-developed sense of what she hoped to learn something about. In the process of selecting her site Susan encountered problems gaining access at some schools that looked interesting. She also made some analytic decisions. For instance, she had to decide: Where would she be most likely to observe reader identity? What classes should she look at? What age students should she observe? At what age would reader identity become observable? When did reader identity begin to matter for kids? Susan chose to observe middle-school students at a private Christian school. Merely by selecting this as a site, she had begun to answer some of the analytic questions posed here.

As the project progressed past the initial site selection and early data collection phases, Susan continued to bring her questions and hunches from her own experience and the literature into conversation with what she was seeing. She did so through writing observer comments in her field notes and by drafting three thoughtful memos (more on memos shortly). She came to class prepared, having reflected on what she was seeing at her site and recalling what she wanted to learn, talking with her critical friends group (more on that soon), and e-mailing and calling me as much as she could reasonably do so. She worked through her ideas and gained greater clarity on what she wanted to learn about reader identity and what she would be able to learn at her site. Analytic questions arose and decisions were made throughout the project, right up until Susan turned in her final report. Throughout the life of the project, Susan used all tools available to her to bring her own thoughts, hunches, experiences, and insights from the literature into conversation with her site and data, making analytic decisions along the way.

Greater clarity regarding what it all means comes when you work to understand the meaning of your data in relation to your research question or research focus. Students begin to do this through writing observer comments that are analytic in nature in their field notes. They try to make sense of what they are seeing in the field and write about it in their field notes in observer comments. The researcher's focus becomes clearer as she spends more time at the site and accumulates more field experiences. The focus also becomes clearer as the researcher forces herself to make sense of make meaning of what she is seeing through these analytic observer comments. In addition to these ongoing analytic activities that occur during data collection, there are other tools at your disposal.

Phone a Friend

Like participants under hot lights with sweaty palms on the game show *Who Wants to Be a Millionaire*, you too can, and should, phone a friend for help. It can make all the difference. In fact, creating a cadre of critical friends and colleagues who will take a hard look at your work and ask good questions is a crucial implement in the ethnographer's toolkit. I recommend that every researcher develop a group of "critical friends"—sometimes this is called a dissertation group or a writing group. I have belonged to such a group for the last 15 years. Typically such a group will meet every few weeks. Members take turns sharing with one another about what is happening with their research or writing and offer encouragement, consolation, advice, and questions to one another. By sharing experiences we are reminded that we are not the only one with role management problems or the only one having trouble making sense of what we are seeing or deciding what to observe. Rather, we share insights and strategies with others. Critical friends suggest different ways of making sense of the data that are being collected. I have found this kind of collegial interaction to be critical to my research.

In order to create such a group all that is required is a desire to meet regularly and to share problems and insights from your research and writing. It helps if everyone is doing some form of qualitative study. It also helps if you can meet regularly. It is critical that you trust these people enough to share your ethnographic foibles and to be able to speak frankly and with kindness and understanding to one another. Usually the groups begin with everyone having a set amount of time to bring an issue or concern to the group and to update them on what is happening at the site or with their writing about the site. The person "presenting" then focuses on a specific issue or problem for which they are seeking advice. I would plan on no less than 40 minutes for a four- to five-member group and no more than 90 minutes, as people have a hard time maintaining focus after that length of time. Often the questions of these critical friends push the research in a useful or positive direction in the study under consideration.

In addition to a formal group meeting I also find it helpful to literally phone a friend. There are many times when I pick up the phone and ask a single colleague for advice on a specific immediate problem. A key informant is not returning calls and e-mails, what should I do? I can't decide if the research question is really about A or B, how can I figure this out? I also frequently call colleagues and invite them to meet me for coffee. These informal interactions where I can muse about what is happening with my project(s) and hear about their research are very helpful. In addition to talking with others, memos are another useful tool in order to make sense of what you are seeing.

What Is a Memo?

One of the most helpful tools you can use as a qualitative researcher is the analytic memo. Memos are another tool we use to interrogate the relationship between what we want to learn and what we are seeing in the field.

Memoing is a procedure used by qualitative researchers for explaining or elaborating on the observations made in the field or for elaborating on the coded categories that the researcher develops in analyzing data. Memos capture the thoughts of the researcher while she is engaged in the process of data collection and analysis. Memos are usually conceptual in nature. They vary in length from one paragraph to several pages. Memos are usually written to oneself, though I have often found it useful to imagine I am writing to a colleague or critical friend. Creating an "audience" or reader for the memo helps me to write them and to be more explicit when I write. The content of memos can include (this listing is in no way exhaustive): commentary on the meaning of an event or of an observation, explanation of a sense of a developing pattern in the data, or identification of areas where more data needs to be collected. They can also be used to further describe some specific aspect of a setting or phenomenon.

I use memos to think through what is happening in the field, to pose questions to myself, and to test out hunches about what is going on in the field. They are also very useful when you have left the field and are trying to make sense of the data as you focus more exclusively on analysis. Memoing is the process whereby I try to push my question forward. I try to reconcile the data that I have been collecting and what I have been learning with my research questions. They help me to explicitly bring my data into conversation with the analytic thoughts running through my mind.

Some typical questions that I find I try to answer in my memos are (again, not an exhaustive listing):

- Are my data enabling me to answer my research questions?
- What kinds of hunches do I have about my research questions?
- What is going on at the site that piques my interest?
- Why do I think X is happening?
- What type of school/person/organization/interaction/place am I observing?
- What is the structure of the thing I am observing?

Sometimes getting started on a memo, especially your first one, can be very daunting. You are being asked to state your ideas and hunches openly and that is, at times, very threatening. While you may have some ideas about what you are seeing at the site, it can be hard to state them openly. In addition, some beginning researchers do not feel that it is their "right" or prerogative to make such judgments or draw conclusions about what they are seeing. I see these concerns as similar to a writer trying to find their voice. The researcher needs to find a way to get beyond these impediments to drawing preliminary conclusions or stating hypotheses. One must find a way to begin.

One of the best ways to get started is just to start writing. What do you see at your site that is interesting? What do you think about it? What questions do you have about it? One of the most helpful explanations of memos that I have heard came from Ray Maietta, founder and principal of Research Talk, a consulting firm that specializes in working with qualitative researchers. Ray identified three types of memos that provide a very useful way to think about the purpose of memos and how they can help you push your project forward in a variety of ways: (1) Points of Curiosity, (2) What I Have Learned So Far, and (3) Methods.

Points of Curiosity memos answer questions such as: What is interesting? Troublesome? Intriguing? These memos can explore an idea that is emerging from the data, a difficulty the researcher is having in the field, or simply a curious event from data collection. These types of memos are motivated by a specific interest or curiosity and can relate to prior knowledge and literature.

The second kind of memo is more global in nature. What have I learned so far? This form of memo requires the researcher to reflect on the project overall to date. It can catalog everything the researcher has learned, or it can focus on a specific learning. It is reflective in nature and offers a summary of learnings. It is usually helpful to end these types of memos by posing the new or reformulated questions that result.

The last type of memo is related to research methods. Researchers often neglect to write down what they actually did while they were in the field. They usually wrote a plan for the project at the start as part of a proposal for funding or a dissertation or class proposal, but then the researcher heads into the field and starts collecting data and making decisions. For instance, rather than interviewing six people as planned, it makes more sense to interview eight; rather than visiting the site once a week as planned, it makes more sense to go twice a week. We reformulate our research question slightly. These types of changes are part and parcel of collecting data in the real world. Changes happen. We make decisions based on the goals of the project as we understand them at the time. The problem is that we often forget to write down these changes and the rationale behind them. The frequency with which these changes should be noted depends on the rhythm of the project, the number of times the researcher is collecting data each week, the overall length of the project, et cetera. In my experience, it is necessary to write a brief methodological memo every couple of weeks.

The methodology memo means you are taking time to take stock of what you have actually done as opposed to what you planned to do, and most importantly, writing out the rationale for these changes. Rather than trying to reconstruct from memory what you actually did when you go to write up and publish your results, you will be able to draw on this trail of memos. Creating a methodological audit trail will make writing your article, report, or final paper easier.

So memos are critical to your process of analysis. They are the place where you sort out what you think is happening and what it might mean. In memos you can take stock of what you have learned and catalog methodological changes and the rationale for them. Making time to write memos is one of the best ways to help yourself be ready when it is time to leave the field and begin the process of more detailed analysis and writing. The act of writing out these thoughts alone often uncovers heretofore unrecognized patterns or detail. The memos also provide you with a very useful written start for your final report or paper when you leave the field and turn exclusively to analysis and writing. Finally, as I'll discuss later in this chapter, in this form of research, writing is, in fact, the primary analytic tool at our disposal.

Theory Is Your Friend

While there are exceptions, I have found that most graduate students are afraid of theory. They say they do not "like theory." Whatever the reason, I find that many students are stymied by theory; they do not seem to know quite what to do with it and see it as an obstacle that they need to get around. I think students are stymied by theory because it is diffuse and often poorly taught. I also think it's because the language surrounding theory is often, though not always, unnecessarily dense and inaccessible. Yet its role is critically important, especially for qualitative researchers. Unless we want every piece of our research to stand on its own, an unconnected island of information or findings without any overarching meaning, we need to learn to use theory. Broadly conceived, theory provides a way of organizing the information you find in the world. Thus, when a researcher is having a hard time seeing the meaning in the data she has collected, it can often be useful to revisit the theoretical notions that led to the exploration in the first place. Does what you are seeing fit with the view predicted by a particular theoretical approach? How? Do some parts fit and others not as much? Why?

Years ago when I was trying to think about how to begin talking about coding and searching for a way to illustrate the basic principles, I developed an exercise that used the Halloween candy that my then young children had recently collected. I like this example, which I will describe below, because almost every student that I have encountered could relate to it in a visceral sort of way as they remembered dressing up as witches or zombies. The exercise is simple. I walk around the circle of desks in which the students sit with a big bag of Halloween candy that is on loan from my children. Everyone takes a big handful. I then ask them to sort or "code" the candy. This activity usually generates some humorous comments and smiles as well as requests to eat the candy, which get a firm "No" as I promised to return all of the candy to my children. Sometimes I get a blank stare: "What do you mean?" they ask. I tell them to sort it in any way they like. If further explanation is required I say that when I was a kid and we would arrive home with our bulging pillowcases of Halloween candy the first thing we would do was to sit on the floor and sort it. By this point no more explanation is needed.

Some people sort into two piles—chocolate and non-chocolate or what to keep and what to give away or use to trade with. Others have more elaborate schemes. They sort according to color or candy type or shape. They sort according to brand or size, and almost always a new sorting strategy emerges that I have not seen before. Then I ask students to explain why they have coded their candy as they have. One student said that she was part of a large family. Fierce trading with siblings was a complicated and lengthy process, so sorting into what to hold onto and what to trade was important. Others talked about what their parents would and would not let them eat. Still others talked about their affinity for chocolate. The point is that everyone had a reason for coding in the way that they did. Though this may be overly simplistic, I suggest that this reasoning that drives the way my students code their candy is not unlike the way that theory can inform research, especially analysis.

Like an affinity for chocolate, or knowing you can trade candy with siblings, theory provides a framework for looking at your data. Theoretical beliefs and assumptions guide your exploration in the field and the way that you make sense of the data you collect. Susan, the student interested in reader identity from earlier in the chapter, had reason to believe, based on prior knowledge and theories about identity, that reader identity is affected by context. Therefore, she designed her study to look across contexts. When it came to analysis, Susan returned to her understanding of identity and reading to develop ideas about how to look at her data. Ultimately she developed a coding scheme that allowed her to sort her data into a few different "buckets" that explored some of these theoretical beliefs as well as into buckets that emerged from her data themselves, like the role of specific teachers. Your beliefs and prior knowledge about what you have found and why it is interesting provide the theoretical foundation for your coding.

Because this is a book for beginners, I provide this very simple explanation of the role of theory. Others have written more and far more eloquently on theory and its role in qualitative research. Indeed, theory development and testing are key goals of most qualitative research, so it makes sense to develop your understanding of the role of theory and to explore your own theoretical stance. We cannot cover it all here, but what is important as a beginner is that you understand that theory constitutes a way of seeing the world, it is linked to epistemology (the way we construct knowledge about the world), and it informs how you go about collecting and analyzing your data (method). Hesse-Biber and Leavy (2006) call this the "research nexus" and provide an excellent extended discussion of it in their textbook on this topic. Try not to be put off by theory. It is essential to your exploration of social spaces and is an indispensable analytic tool.

Drawing a Picture

Drawing a picture of your site or project can be another useful analytic tool. Much of the work that we do in school is linear and written. We write papers, reports, and memos. We endeavor to make coherent linear arguments. Many of us have been doing this for years as we have moved through school. And yet, one of the most useful tools for students in my class as they try to make sense of what is happening at their site is nonlinear. As part of the unit on analysis, I ask students to draw a picture of their site—any sort of sketch, drawing, or representation that makes sense to them. Though the start is usually tentative and some students express a lack of comfort with drawing, I reassure students that we are not interested in artistic talent. At times representing their site in a different way can lead to uncovering hidden relationships or meaning. The results vary greatly, from stick figures representing people at a site to process flowcharts to a literal likeness of a place to a map. After about 10 minutes, I ask if anyone would like to share their drawing. Usually only one tentative hand goes up.

The brave student who has volunteered comes to the front of the room and draws her picture on the whiteboard. We talk about it. We ask questions. Why did you draw this person bigger than everyone else? Why do the arrows only go one way in your concept map? What is the relationship between these two ideas or people? The sense of excitement and engagement in the room grows. The artist/researcher explains the drawing and then as questions are asked often begins erasing and redrawing certain parts or changes the drawing in some way. Sometimes a classmate hops up and adds something to the drawing. The author/researcher often pauses the conversation to say, "Oh wait, I have to write this down!" as she has some new understanding about what is going on or how to look at her data. I ask for a second volunteer and all the hands go up. Drawing, doodling, and making charts and maps of our data can be very useful analytic tools.

Sharing Data and Emergent Analysis with Participants

Another tool or analytic strategy that is used at times is to share emergent analysis with study participants, but I strongly caution novice researchers against this strategy. There are many pitfalls to doing this (see Lareau, 2011, for an extended exploration of some of them). Save this tool for much later in your career.

GETTING STARTED WITH THE ACTUAL WRITING

So you have written memos, drawn a picture of your site, and talked over your ideas with colleagues. You say, "Okay, so these tools are helpful and I can see how I have been doing analysis all along. But now that I am done collecting data and really just need to analyze what I've got, how do I start? What do I do?"

The best way to start is to first make sure your data are ready to be analyzed. If you have done interviews and recorded them, they will need to be transcribed. Some researchers feel that they gain valuable insight from transcribing their own interviews. I disagree with this viewpoint as I find the process so tedious and slow, perhaps because my typing skills are so limited. If you are doing it yourself, you will need to allow ample time for transcription. Transcription is *very* time-consuming and tedious. If you do it yourself it does allow you to reexperience your data and listen to it as you transcribe. This benefit of doing it yourself is good for beginners, but for the experienced researcher in my opinion, marginal. If you have the resources to pay for someone else to transcribe your interviews, it is worth the money later in your career.

In addition to having interviews transcribed, you need to make sure your field notes are in good order. It helps if you have followed a consistent format. If you collected documents, they need to be brought together and perhaps organized. Your memos, notes, and anything else you collected needs to be all in one place, ready for you to look at. It is often helpful to design a chart or two or table that summarizes all of your data. The process of doing this is an important analytic step and can lead to new understanding about your data. It can allow you to see where you may have gaps in your data. For instance, you may realize that you have far fewer interviews with individuals in one demographic category than another. Or you may realize that, in fact, you did attend every meeting of a particular group, creating a complete record of that year's meetings.

Once you have all of your data, the best thing to do is to read it. That's right, read it. While you may have some ideas of things you want to code for, you need to read all of your data before diving in. I usually sit down with the data and a blank pad of paper. I write out all of the areas I know that I want to code for or that are important to the project. These codes are drawn from theory and the literature that I may have already read on the topic, and they are usually things that drew me to the study in the first place. For instance, I am often interested in social capital—a theoretical concept that frequently guides my inquiry. I usually code my data for this construct.[1] Then, I begin reading. I make notes in the margins of the transcripts and highlight and underline things that look interesting. Sometimes I know why something is interesting and I will give it a name that describes its importance to the study or research question. Other times I do not know why I think a particular piece of data is interesting—but I know that it is interesting. That is enough for now. I write thoughts and ideas on the pad along with questions that come up. And I keep reading.

Once I have read either a substantial amount of the data or the entire data corpus, I write a memo about what I think is interesting and what I think is going on. I explore relationships and pose questions. This leads to the development of other codes in addition to the ones I wrote down when I started. I write a draft coding scheme similar to the example included here in Figure 5.1 (p. 116), which presents a draft coding scheme we developed to analyze the 57 interviews my colleague James Davis and I conducted as a part of the YouthBuild national study. We published the results from this study in 2011 (Horvat & Davis, 2011). This coding scheme is an initial draft. Some of the codes, such as transition to school or work, as well as barriers to completing the program, were of specific interest to YouthBuild. James and I were interested in capturing the changes in students' lives and outlooks that occurred while in the program. Finally, some of the codes emerged from the data themselves, including the impact that YouthBuild had on graduates' life expectancy, the role of faith in their lives, and the role their children played in motivating change.

Once I have a draft coding scheme I develop a working definition of each code. The task here is to define the code in such a way that when I go through the data to code it I will be able to determine what belongs in each code and what does not. This is especially important when you are working as a part of a team or if someone else is doing the coding for you, as was the case on the YouthBuild project. Defining each code provides a more detailed explanation of what I am actually looking for in the data to put into this

Figure 5.1. Sample Draft Coding Scheme

YouthBuild—National Qualitative Graduate Study

DRAFT: Coding Scheme

Demographics

- Number of Years Past Graduation
- Age
- Gender
- Race
- Kids while in YB
- Currently Working or in School
- Program Site

Conceptual Codes

Support While in Program
From Program
From Others
From Parent Type Person

Manhood
Womanhood
Fatherhood
Motherhood

Independence/Yet Needing Support
Schooling
Learning Issues

Street Life
Drug Dealer
Drug User (Self)
Drug Use (Family/friends)

Criminal Justice
Jail
Prison
Parole

YouthBuild as a Life-Changing
    Experience
Significant Event
Care/Love
Parents
Violence
Staff
Community Service
Mental Toughness
Responsibility
High Expectations
Abuse
Sexual
General
Respect
Housing/Living Situations

Education as a Credential
    (HS Diploma/GED/College)
Leadership
Building/Construction
Mental Health

category. In my case, it makes explicit the implicit definitions of each code that I have developed based on my understanding of the topic and my initial reading of the data. Figure 5.2 (pp. 118–121) presents an example of a draft set of definitions drawn again from the YouthBuild study.

Once I have a good working coding scheme with definitions of the codes, I then sit down with the data and start coding. I usually do this again with just a pen and paper copies of the data. I get through a substantial portion of the data in this way—with just a pen—and then go back and review what I have done. Have any new codes emerged? Are there new ideas about the data? Do the codes that I am using make sense? I make adjustments to the coding scheme and then start in earnest. It is important to note here that while at this point I usually consider the coding scheme to be "set"—that is, I am fairly certain that I will be able to capture what I want to using it, I remain open to adding codes, collapsing two codes into one, and making other adjustments as I progress. Analysis is a process of finding the meaning in the data. As a result, the researcher is best served by remaining open to developments and changes as the process progresses. As I proceed through this process of analysis and become more certain of what the data are telling me, changes or adjustments to the coding scheme become less frequent.

FROM COLORED PENCILS TO ANALYTIC SOFTWARE

What do I mean when I say I start in earnest? Well, it depends. On early small projects I literally used colored pencils. I would start with a clean set of the data in hard copy and draw colored lines around text. Other ethnographers I know used to cut up their transcripts and field notes and paste them onto cards and sort them into categories. Many dining room tables and living room floors have been covered with stacks of data. Over the years people have used all kinds of techniques to sort their data into meaningful categories. Most people now use computer software to accomplish this task.

The categories that you develop and the way in which you code data into these categories will vary from one study to the next. The type of data and how much data winds up in each bucket or code varies. If you are observing the micro-aggressions that occur between 2nd-grade girls on a playground, your units of data will look very different than if you are interested in the development of state education policy. The unit of analysis—the thing you are interested in being able to say something about—varies from one study to the next. In the type of studies I conduct, I usually find myself coding a few sentences of an interview or a paragraph of field notes at a time. If I was interested in more fine-grained units, I might be coding in smaller chunks. In some studies, each word that a participant uses may be

text continues on p. 122

Figure 5.2. Sample Draft Coding Scheme with Definitions

YouthBuild—National Qualitative Graduate Study

DRAFT: Coding Scheme and Definitions

Demographics

- Age
- Gender
- Race
- Parental Status
- Currently Working or in School
- Program Site

Conceptual Codes

Support While in Program

Anything having to do with how the student felt supported while in the program.
Includes: financial, emotional, and other types of support.
From Program
From Others
From Parent Type Person

Manhood
Womanhood
Fatherhood
Motherhood

The above codes will include any reference to the way in which students became or acted as men and women (as opposed to children or adolescents) or saw themselves as a grown man or woman. We are interested in the gendered differences here and the kinds of experiences that are different for men and women, hence we did not use the terms "adult" or "parent."

Independence/Yet Needing Support

In the above code we are interested in capturing those instances where graduates explore growing independence or the role of independence in their lives (independent too early at times) and also need for further support. We are especially interested in the tension between these two concepts—wanting and exhibiting independence and yet also needing further support.

Schooling

Anything having to do with traditional school: attendance, like/dislike of school, activities at school, teachers, peers, and so on.

Figure 5.2. Sample Draft Coding Scheme with Definitions *(continued)*

Dropping Out of School

We asked most students to describe how they stopped going to school. All of that information should be captured here—even if it is not a typical "dropout" story.

Learning Issues

Any issues having to do with their ability to learn. Many graduates talked about problems learning and reading, and so forth, or ways in which school did not work with them or learning deficits that they came to YB with. Many graduates also talked about special talents or skills they had—subjects they were good at or liked. These can be captured here.

Street Life

Many graduates talked about the ways in which the life of the street, including violence, drug use, drug dealing, and gangs, influenced their lives before, during, and after YB. General information on the street life can be captured in this code, and specific information on drug use, dealing, and drug involvement of friends and family can be captured with the codes below.

Drug Dealer (self or family and friends)
Drug User (self)
Drug Use (family/friends)

Criminal Justice

Information in involvement with the criminal justice system can be divided into the four categories below.

Jail
Prison
Parole
Juvenile

YouthBuild as a Life-Changing Experience

Many graduates talked about YB as a significant or life-changing experience. These statements can be captured in this code.

Significant Event

In many graduates' lives there were pivotal, crucial, or significant life events. Many times the graduates identified these events as significant and at items they did not. Any event that the researcher feels is significant or that is identified as significant should be placed here. Examples of such events include jail or prison time, birth of a child, and connecting with a teacher/adult in a special way.

Care/Love

Any reference to the presence or absence of care and love in the lives of the graduates should be placed in this code.

Figure 5.2. Sample Draft Coding Scheme with Definitions *(continued)*

Parents

Any information on the parents' presence or absence in the lives of the graduates or their effect on the graduate should go here.

Violence

Any reported instances of violence either in the family, on the streets, or elsewhere should go here. Many of these items will likely be double-coded with abuse and street life.

Staff

Any references to YB staff.

Community Service

Any reference to community service work completed within or outside of the program or its impact on the graduate.

Mental Toughness

Any reference to the mental toughness training that students undergo.

Responsibility

Any reference to responsibility in the lives of the graduates.

High Expectations

Any reference to high expectations held by the staff or others for them when they were students or after such as an employer.

Abuse

Any reference to abuse of any type needs to be coded. Please divide the abuse into sexual and general. Abuse can include violence and sexual abuse but it can also include neglect and other types of abuse as well.
Sexual
General

Respect

Any reference to respect for self or others or others respecting the graduate.

Housing/Living Situations

Any information on the housing or living situation of graduates before, during, and after YB.

Education as a Credential (HS Diploma/GED/College)

Any reference to the power of education as a credential.

Leadership

Any reference to the presence or absence of leadership skills or development among students and graduates.

Figure 5.2. Sample Draft Coding Scheme with Definitions *(continued)*

Building/Construction

Any reference to the building and construction aspect of the program.

Mental Health

Many graduates mentioned mental health issues within their families or with themselves. All references should be captured here.

What could YB do for you now?

Any suggestions as to what YB could do for graduates should be coded here.

Race/Racism

Any commentary about race/racism or reported instances of racism and discrimination in YouthBuild and beyond.

Faith/Religion/Spirituality

References to religious faith, belief in God, or spiritual acknowledgment and awareness of a higher power.

Money/Finances

Any reference to money or financial matters.

Aspiration and Dreams

Many graduates talked about their hopes, aspirations, and dreams—before, after, and during YouthBuild. These statements should be reflected in this code.

Family

Any information related to family members and the presence/effect of family on the lives of graduates.

Peers/YouthBuild Peer Experiences

Any reference to peers or interaction with peers in and outside of YouthBuild.

Work/Job/Employment

Any statement about work and job-related experiences. These statements may pertain to pre- or post-YouthBuild employment.

YouthBuild Program/Academic Experiences

Many graduates talked about their experiences in YouthBuild, including academic and program experiences. These statements should *not* include references to building and construction experiences.

Future

Any reference to future plans of any type should be coded here. Future may include statements about jobs/employment, professional, and personal matters after YB. Future items may be double-coded with Aspirations and Dreams.

important. In other studies entire policy reports may be representative of a particular coding category. The size of the chunks of data that you code and the meaning of those chunks of data will be determined by the specifics of each study.

Whether you are using colored pencils or computer software, and whether the chunks of data you code are words, sentences, or paragraphs, the process is the same. You begin placing your data into categories. In earlier stages of analysis when I mark up transcripts in the margins and write notes I am not as certain about the analytic categories, but after working with the data and developing a coding scheme I begin to have a sense of comfort with the codes, know what I want in each one, and more confidently place data in each code. This does not mean that new codes cannot emerge or that you will never have to backtrack; you will. As you code your data, patterns will emerge. You will realize that you have lots of data in some areas and very little in others.[2] I usually begin at this point to get very angry with myself for not collecting a particular kind of data or asking a specific question in interviews. But I also can get very excited as I begin to see the treasure trove that I have collected. I try to write memos and notes as I code to document themes and ideas that emerge.

At the end of the coding phase of your study you will have gone through all of your data and placed all relevant pieces of data into codes. Does this mean that every word or every piece of data you have collected gets placed into a code? No, there will be some data that you have collected that does not get coded. It could be that some data you collected turns out to be irrelevant to your study. It is also often the case that there are some pieces of data that are important to the overall context of the study and you needed to record them, but they are not conceptually important enough to warrant placing into a code.

So my data are coded, what now? More reading and writing. At this point all of your data, or a great deal of it, has been dumped, either electronically or manually, into different buckets or piles. Now you have to figure out what each pile means. Let's return to our friend Susan. Susan knew that she was interested in reader identity and context, so she coded for everything that she thought indicated a student had an identity as a reader: field note excerpts where she noted they were carrying novels, times when they read at recess, interview transcripts where teachers talked about students being readers, et cetera. Susan had a lot of data in this category. But what did it mean? The task now is to bring these data excerpts into conversation with your research question again. Susan had to look at all of the data in this category again and try to understand what she could learn from it about reader identity and context. So she read the data in each code and then began to write about it. Susan had coded her data into categories related to reader identity: definition of a reader, reader activities, reader habits, reading choices, and talk about reading in classroom and out-of-school contexts. What do the data tell her about how reader identity changes across different classroom contexts? In Susan's case she figured this out by writing memos, talking with me and her critical friends, and thinking about her data and her question. Often, writing about the data is another analytic step.

WRITING IS ANALYSIS

Often we do not understand how important writing is to the analytic process in qualitative research. We expect we will code our data and then be able to turn out a reasonable draft of our paper. In reality, writing is a critical part of the analytic process. It is through writing the story of what we have learned that we actually figure out what we have learned.

In my class, for example, I require a full rough draft of each student's' final paper to be turned in 3 weeks prior to the final paper due date. At first my students do not understand why they need to write a rough draft. Some even anticipate an early end to the work of the class. "How much work could there possibly be in revising a rough draft?" they think. Most students are not accustomed to working on several drafts of a paper before turning it in. Maybe they get the paper done one day before its due date and do some editing. Usually, that's about it. By requiring a complete draft so far in advance I signal to students that I expect that they will revise the draft. Indeed this draft is read by me, my teaching assistant, and two "critical friends" from the class. All four readers provide both written and oral feedback. We devote one class meeting to critiquing papers and all students have an individual appointment with me the following week to determine what changes need to be made to their paper. What students begin to understand through this process is that the first draft is usually what one of my graduate school professors called "the data dump." The first draft is just for getting your ideas on paper. And getting those ideas on paper is a critical part of the analytic process—but only a first step.

Turning out a paper that actually tells a story with the data, one that explains what has been learned about a particular process, people, or place, takes more than one draft. It is through the writing and revising of drafts that researchers often come to see what the data are saying to them and how it relates to what they set out to learn. And, as Bradley Bergey describes in the next chapter, it requires that some fun or compelling parts of the story get edited out so that the central idea can shine brightly.

Most beginner researchers have little experience conducting their own studies and writing them up. We have experience only as "consumers" or readers of research articles, reports, and books. We are accustomed to reading the finished products of others and have little understanding of how these products are produced. While methods sections in articles and books provide some detail as to how the research was done, these versions are usually somewhat sanitized or cleaned-up versions of what really happened in the study and offer only a summary of how the study was conducted rather than a detailed blow-by-blow account. Like the "man behind the curtain" in *The Wizard of Oz*, researchers pull many levers and turn many dials in order to conduct high-quality research and write publication-worthy reports of their findings. They work hard to produce a report that appears to support their conclusions seamlessly and logically. In reality, the process of conducting most studies and producing a well-crafted final report or paper is far less seamless and much messier than we are often led to believe. Studies are full of twists and turns, with the researcher often doubling back to reconsider data or revise the coding scheme as he or she inches toward conclusions that can be supported by the data. This messy process is, like the man behind the curtain, hidden from view in the final product.

In the account above I have provided a detailed road map of the twists and turns that one can expect to encounter on the path to producing a polished ethnographic report. While the exact journey of every researcher is different, it is usually true that we are well served by beginning our analytic process early by writing frequent memos during data collection and by using the other tools identified here. It is also true that polished reports or papers are not "one and done" affairs. Writing is a critical part of the analytic process where we work out ideas. In addition, good writing usually requires multiple drafts. In the end, I am convinced that qualitative researchers are as much craftspeople as they are scientists. They must be familiar with the tools of their trade and learn to artfully apply their skill in order to produce a polished product.

NOTES

1. I conceive of social capital as connections and trust among individuals. So, for instance, when I code I look for connections among parents at a school site and expressions of trust among these parents.

2. You may also realize that one piece of data can be coded in two or three different categories. Typically I allow data to be coded into more than one category—or to be labeled with two or three different codes. In my mind this reflects the complexity of lived experience and the degree to which actions and words can have multiple meanings. If, however, you find yourself coding every piece of data with many multiple codes or coding pieces of data with five and six codes, this may mean your coding scheme is not working well and should be revisited.

ERIN HORVAT

In this chapter, Bradley Bergey, a 2nd-year doctoral student, tells the tale of his ethnographic journey. He focuses on how he struggled to settle on a question for his project. Bradley had done a good bit of thinking about questions, their nature, and development prior to embarking on this study. In this chapter he explores the relationship among question development, data collection, and crafting an answer to his research question. He describes how his question developed while he acquired his own set of "ethnographic eyes" as a researcher and how he worked to settle on a question that was answerable given the time frame (one semester), resources, and data he had to work with.

As a former middle and high school teacher Bradley had spent considerable time wondering about the questions his students asked. Why did some of his students ask questions and others did not? What led a student to ask a question at a particular moment in time? What were students' concerns in asking a question? When he entered graduate school he began to explore this topic in the literature and through projects in his classes. When he began his first qualitative project he knew, therefore, that it would focus on student questions. What he came to learn is that the development of his own question for this particular project would take time as he learned what types of research questions he might actually be able to answer and which aspects of student question development were of greatest interest to him.

As Bradley details in the chapter, the selection of the site for this study is slightly unusual, because the site was not completely novel. As I noted elsewhere, it is generally not a good idea to observe where you work or in a site that is overly familiar to you. In this case Bradley was observing a professor he knew well at his own university. This class offered a potentially interesting design that would have been hard to find elsewhere: It is one of the few at the university that blends online student participation with live student participation. Initially Bradley was very interested in the difference between questions asked online and in class. In addition, he argued, he would be able to gain access to the questions students posed via e-mail, as this particular professor agreed to allow him access to these questions. The opportunity to examine question-asking in this variety of modalities presented a compelling opportunity, one that seemed to outweigh the risk of being overly familiar with the site and the participants. While this aspect of Bradley's project turned out not to provide the rich variety of question-asking strategies that he had hoped for, and the difference between online and live student questions did not remain his focus, at the outset this design appeared to offer a unique opportunity that warranted making an exception to my "rule."

In developing the focus for his study Bradley describes three "blindnesses" that he passed through on the way to settling on his research question. After first being unable to see what was interesting or noteworthy in the class he was observing, Bradley became "blinded" by all of the possible questions he could ask. Like a man coming out of the desert, he was overwhelmed by the water everywhere. Though flooded with possible research questions, he realized that part of settling on the right question is allowing other very good questions to go unanswered for the present. As Bradley describes this journey he provides insight into the important relationship among the data that have been collected, the many questions that could be asked and answered, and the interest and goals of the researcher. Along the way Bradley also allows us to share in his hopes and fears for his project and the way in which he learned to move through them as he developed skill as a qualitative researcher.

Three Times Blind

The Wandering, Wondering Path to Asking the Right Question

Bradley W. Bergey

WHAT'S IN A (RESEARCH) QUESTION?

Everybody asks questions. From the moment we acquire the most tenuous grasp of language, we begin interrogating the people and things that fill our world. Young children begin to ask what objects are called and what the words they hear mean, and then, as they begin to understand causality, an interminable string of *why* questions fills the air. As we grow up, we become more sophisticated in what, how, and why we ask questions, and they are such an integral part of our daily experience that we often pay them little mind.

Yet questions are a unique aspect of human speech and thought. They differ in important ways from making a declarative statement, for example. In voicing a question, we provide an explicit invitation to others in our environment to respond to our query. By seeking information from our environment, askers uniquely interact and engage their surroundings. In posing a question, we seek information that we know we do not know. In this sense, questions are metacognitive—they are thinking about our thinking. In our daily life, we often experience questions spontaneously. They "pop" into our heads. They "occur" to us. With a *poof*, they appear in our thoughts. In many ways, questions seem to happen *to* us, the product of some magical unconscious chemistry between attention, thinking, and interest. We bring these experiences of asking questions to our research endeavors, and in some ways are naturally well prepared for asking questions in the field.

However, posing a research question differs in important ways from how we normally generate questions. First of all, articulating research questions is a deliberate act. They rarely "pop" into our heads in polished form. When we enter the field to conduct qualitative research, we are often tasked with *finding* our research question. Far from the passive spontaneity of questioning in informal settings, in the field we *pursue* questions. We rustle the bushes of what we experience in the hopes of scaring questions from their hidden dens. Once they are loosed, we track them, observing how they perform over time. The questions we initially generate are rarely the questions we ultimately pose as research questions. Instead, we reshape them, clipping and bending words and ideas. In the end, we do not—we cannot—ask them all. We must select our research question from the alternatives. To do so, we must consider a variety of factors, including what we find most interesting, most important, most useful, and most feasibly answered with our data. In this sense, the question is shaped both by the desire to know what is not known and the act of discovering what is becoming known. The act of asking a question is entangled with our ongoing evaluation of our ability to answer it.

THE STARTING POINT

When I agreed to participate in this book, I was heartened by the fact that I was chosen because I was an amateur—perhaps a competent amateur on many points, but assuredly and consistently an amateur. As a 2nd-year educational psychology doctoral student, I am an ethnographer the way a child learning to ride a tricycle is a cyclist—that is, tentatively, swervingly, with furrowed brow, scraped knees, and a whole lot of help. I trust that if a reader learns from this chapter it will be as likely from my mistakes as from my successes.

Of course, amateurs have more to offer than their blunders—any professional can talk you to sleep with their own list of challenges, shortcomings, and lessons learned. Amateurs bring something unique. Our learning about the process of doing ethnography is fresh. This allows us a unique perspective on the experience. Because experts interpret the world through highly organized and elaborate schema, it can be difficult at times for them to imagine the world through the less elaborate, more poorly organized schema of novices. That is, their expertise can blind them from seeing the task of doing ethnography the way you and I—people just learning the craft—see it. My hope, therefore, is that you find something useful from reading about the recent experience of a fellow amateur, who fumbled and floundered his way through the process, but who ultimately survived and enjoyed it.

I start my description of this process with a metaphor—how my experience of searching for a research question was analogous to iterative stages of seeing and blindness. Then, I will describe the chain of choices that characterized my experience collecting and analyzing data about graduate students' questioning behavior in an introductory statistics course. I detail how I arrived at the research site, how I collected observational and interview data, and how these data influenced the research questions I asked. I will end by discussing my initial hopes and fears for the project.

THRICE BLINDED: A METAPHOR

For me, the deliberative act of seeking, posing, and deciding on research questions was challenging and disorienting. Since knowing is a form of "seeing" meaning in one's environment, vision seems like an apt metaphor for describing my struggle pursuing a research question. I say *pursue* because asking a research question was not a singular occurrence; it was a process. For me, the challenge of asking and selecting research questions changed over the course of the project, with each step uniquely illuminating and straining my vision. Over the course of the semester, I felt as if I had been blinded three times. For each step, I found strategies that helped me restore clarity of vision.

The First Blindness

Imagine stepping into a dark room. You are immediately struck by your lack of vision, blinded by the lack of light. The darkness seems suffocatingly close to you, a blanket you cannot see through. Without familiar references, you are disoriented. You feel stillness. You wonder if there is anything to see here, and if there is, how you will ever be able to perceive it.

My first experience in the field was like this—a shocking and disorienting plunge into darkness. In the first minutes, hours, even days in the field, it was difficult to start generating questions about what I was seeing. Even though the sensory-rich environment of a classroom surrounded me, I experienced a distinct mental stillness in which I wondered, *Is there anything to see here? What is worth attending to? What is interesting here? What questions can I ask?* These questions were accompanied by a disconcerting realization that things were not exactly as I imagined them to be. I feared having chosen the wrong research site. I thought it might be better if I backed out of there before things got any worse.

But, like an eye acclimating to lower levels of ambient light, my inability to see and pose research questions was only a temporary state of disorientation, requiring minor adjustments and a bit of patience. My first blindness was cured through exploration. Just as we instinctively use our hands to feel our way through darkness, exploration involved staying close to all of my senses, wondering: What am I hearing and smelling? What nonverbal communication accompanies a spoken message? How is time structured and how do people interact within it?

In class we learned that qualitative research requires a high tolerance for ambiguity. More than tolerate ambiguity, my task during this first blindness was to seed and cultivate ambiguity. My initial blindness was the result of seeing the classroom activities too concretely, too unproblematically, too unambiguously. I saw a professor using PowerPoint slides to teach statistics to students. "What is interesting about this?" I thought. "PowerPoint slides help organize information and provide a record of what was covered during the lecture. What of this is relevant to students' willingness to ask questions?" In that first observation, it did not occur to me to ask, for example, what does it *mean* to teach using PowerPoint slides? I did not wonder, as I would later, how the structured, teacher-driven nature of the course influenced students' perceptions of what it means to "interrupt" with a question. While questioning the meaning of ordinary actions is likely challenging in any environment, it may have been especially challenging for me since I was researching people with whom I was acquainted and in an environment with which I was familiar. In this context, it was easy to make automatic meaning of the actions I was observing. These routine ways of making meanings were the result of my beliefs and assumptions about what happened in the course and what it meant. In order to ask questions in this environment, I needed to disabuse myself of some of the assumptions that shaped the meaning I made so that I could see differently. At this stage in the process, I needed to actively court ambiguity. What initially appeared self-evident needed to be questioned. What was clear at first glance needed to be muddied. What was obvious had to be problematized.

For me, the process of exploring possible meanings was a very productive stage in generating research questions. So many of the actions I observed provoked questions for me. These questions led to others, which led to still others, and so on.

The Second Blindness

Soon, my experience in the field had become quite the opposite. With time, attention, and reflection, I had become flooded with a seemingly endless flow of possible research questions. This was a new type of blindness. I was entertaining so many questions that my vision was clouded by the sheer number of possible directions and enticing leads. There were too many questions to ask, which was disorienting in a different way. In attaching importance to such a wide range of phenomena, I found it difficult to see the most viable path forward. It was the product of seeing the complexity of the multifaceted and interrelated dynamic systems that are present in all social environments. As I became attuned to one question, others came into focus as well. My mind spun with possibilities. There were more questions than could be answered, and each question suggested others.

The Third Blindness

Nobel-winning chemist Linus Pauling once noted that "the way to get good ideas is to get lots of ideas and throw away the bad ones." The same appears to be true for research questions. The best way for me to arrive at a quality research question was to generate many to choose from. This required the difficult task of selecting the best question. This was my third blindness. It is the gradual blinding of myself to other research questions— an intentional restriction of focus.

Rather than throwing out the "bad" questions, the selection process for me was about choosing the *right* question. Or, perhaps, *a* right question, since there may be multiple, viable research questions. But I struggled with knowing which of the many research questions I had generated was the right one. The process involved an ongoing negotiation between my interests, my goals, and my data. These were dynamic components, and aligning them was no easy task.

Interest is an important motivating factor. Qualitative research requires lots of tedious tasks (e.g., transcription), and having a question that I truly cared about did much to buttress my resolve through the arduous process of research. Not all questions were equally interesting to me. For some, my interest waned soon after I had asked the question. Others continued to excite or pester me. By selecting a question which I honestly, urgently, and deeply wanted to know the answer to, my research project became personally meaningful and provided much-needed fuel for the process.

In addition to interest, a right question was one that fit with my goals for the project. I echo Professor Horvat's fondness for unreasonable goals. I hoped to do much with this project, including create a product that I could present at a conference and explore possible dissertation topics. My goals, however, needed to take into account the considerable constraints of time and resources that accompany a semester-long research course. In the end, my research questions reflected what I thought was a reasonably sized question for my circumstance.

Perhaps most importantly, the right question was the one that I could answer with the data I had or could collect. For me, this was the most critical factor as I selected a viable research question. I generated some questions that were tantalizingly interesting to me and fit my goals, but in the end, I did not have the data to answer them. They were destined to remain (at least for now) a question. In the end, I needed to select the question that could be most fully answered with my data in the short time that I had.

In my experience, this selection process involved an interaction among my questions, data, and interests. My interests shaped the data I collected, which, in turn, triggered questions. In response, questions that I generated influenced my interest, which, in turn, shaped the data I collected. My questions evolved as my interests and data evolved. This process, it seems, can be endless; however, my project could not be. In the end, I needed to choose my most viable question and leave the rest for later.

This selection process was surprisingly painful at points. I was excited by the potential I saw in a diverse range of directions. By focusing on a singular research question, I needed to blind myself to other elements in the field that I thought were interesting, valuable, worth studying, and part of the bigger picture. Yet in selecting a research question, this is what we must do, knowing—and being humbled by the knowledge—that we can only tell one story at a time, if we are to tell any of them well.

SELECTING A SITE

The story I chose to tell started with a piece of advice a faculty mentor gave me on selecting a topic and site for a dissertation: "Negotiate between your interests and your opportunities. Balance the ideal with the actual." This advice served me well as I planned this small study. As I considered possible classrooms in which to observe students' questions, I limited myself to courses that were taught at my university. My 20-hour-a-week research assistantship required that I be in one of two high schools during the day. I ruled out these schools as possible sites because I wanted to be able to present, and if possible, publish on the data that I gathered, and knew obtaining parental consent would be an enormous obstacle. I considered working with a colleague, who taught an undergraduate course on Institutional Racism, but the second of two long conversations revealed her concerns about the departmental IRB process[1] and the negative effect a researcher might have on students' willingness to discuss sensitive issues of race. Then my advisor offered me the opportunity to use her class as a site. She taught a semester-long, graduate-level introductory statistics course.

I was initially reluctant to take her up on the offer for several reasons. I thought researching graduate students might limit the usefulness of my findings for others (we are, after all, strange creatures with a unique affinity for formal education). I wondered if learning statistics was somehow too unique of a learning experience (some might say punishment) and had too little relevance to learning in other domains. I had concerns regarding my familiarity with my advisor's teaching and classes. I had taken this course and others with her in previous semesters, and was familiar with the style and structure of her teaching. Would I be able see what was occurring in her classroom with fresh eyes? Furthermore, I was concerned that my close relationship with my advisor might inhibit me from sharing honestly about what I might find. After all, as Professor Horvat cautioned me at the start of the research process, teaching is an intimate act. Was I willing to research in a site in which the subject of my research would also be a reader of it, and one with a good deal of influence on my future? Our relationships with those we research can be complicated and we need to act delicately and reflexively as we navigate these waters, an issue Emily Trancredi-Brice Agbenyega explores in illuminating detail in Chapter 4 of this volume.

In the end, however, the benefits of the site seemed to outweigh the costs. The once-a-week evening class fit nicely into my schedule. More important to my decision, the course had a unique structure that I hoped would allow me to ask interesting and unique research questions. In the weeks before the course began, I explained my thinking to Professor Horvat:

> Professor G's Introduction to Statistics provides a natural experiment that would allow me to investigate some interesting questions. She is teaching one section of the course on Tuesday nights with the lectures streamed live and recorded and archived via [a virtual classroom system]. A second section of the class will be logging in to watch these lectures (either live or using the archived recording). . . . Students—both in the classroom and from satellite locations—may post nonanonymous questions during the live session.
> In addition, Dr. G said that she is willing to save e-mails and to record questions that are asked during office hours. This arrangement allows me to consider question-asking along two different dimensions: public/private and in-person/electronic. Some questions will be asked during class sessions by students who are physically in the classroom [in-person] and others who are online [electronic]; in both cases, the questions are nonanonymous and public (in front of peers). Other questions will be asked privately to the instructor during office hour [in-person] or via e-mail [electronic]. This gives me four quadrants to explore: (1) Public in-person, (2) public electronic, (3) private in-person, and (4) private electronic. This seems like fertile ground to pursue my interests.

At the start of the semester, I fancied myself well positioned for the project and felt secretly prideful about my preparedness. I had a research site locked and loaded. I had a tight research design that allowed me to compare students' questioning between in-person and online students and in private and public environments, creating four tidy quadrants. I had two research questions in hand: What are the social costs of asking a question? and How do online and in-person learning environments inhibit questioning similarly and differently? To top it off, I planned to use the theoretical model of Expectancy-Value Theory[2] to explain it all. The future looked bright.

THE FIRST BLINDNESS

What they say of mice and men and their ill-fated plans also, it appears, applies to researchers, at least novice ones. Despite the nice, clean research design I had planned and my initial research questions, what I found in the field was different than what I imagined. My first few weeks in the field were characterized by trying to adjust to unforeseen limitations and trading imagined notions for verifiable and viable ones.

Several aspects of my orderly design quickly dissolved. First, the in-person class met in a regular classroom, not a computer lab as it had in previous semesters. To my surprise, no students used laptops during the lectures. This meant that only online students would be able to chat questions virtually during class. This reality was coupled with the fact that few online students logged into the virtual classroom system in real time during class meetings. Of the 14 that were enrolled in the online section, the names of only five or six appeared in the chat function interface each week, a number that would shrink to two or three after the midterm exam. These unforeseen circumstances limited my ability to compare in-person and online students' questions during class meetings.

The comparison was further complicated by my inability to gain immediate access to students' e-mails. In order to access private communications between students and the professor—an act that seemed far more invasive than conducting field observations of classroom and online interactions—I felt ethically obliged to obtain IRB approval and students' informed consent. Although I started this process immediately, submitting an application during the 3rd week of the course, I did not receive IRB approval until 5 weeks later. Furthermore, online students rarely attended office hours. Therefore, since I was delayed in gaining access to e-mail, could observe only a small number of online students who logged in synchronously, and saw even fewer students during office hours, I had virtually no access to the online students. It became clear that I could not see what I initially wanted to examine. I had been blinded by preconceived notions of what I would observe in the field.

For the data to which I did have immediate access—students' attending in-person class meetings and office hours—I found myself in the dark as to what I should be paying attention to. Students' questions were my principal interest but these were relatively rare. In one class, students might generate five questions; in another class, eight. In the first 2 weeks, no students attended office hours. The students appeared relatively passive during class meetings—taking notes, watching the professor, flipping through the presentation handouts. In the absence of much student activity, I wondered what concrete observable behaviors in a classroom environment were relevant to question-asking.

As I grasped for something to capture, Professor G became the focus of my initial field observations. I tried to capture everything she was doing that might remotely relate to students' willingness to ask questions. I chronicled how she started class with the precision of a Swiss watch (e.g., "Well, the computer says exactly 5:30 and I'm a firm believer in starting on time"). I documented how she explained terms (e.g., "In everyday language, what does *average* mean?") and remedial concepts (e.g., "If I have one buck and owe you three, I'll have what? Right! Negative two."). I described how she talked about the class and statistics (e.g., "I am a picky grader. This is a picky enterprise.") and what students would be held accountable for (e.g., "I'm not going to ask you much about the numerator, but I will about the denominator"). I noted her attempts at humor (e.g., "In an exaggerated German accent, Dr. G announces, 'Yah, I know how readings verks!'") and how she referenced students' interests (e.g., "Brent might be interested in a measure of general tendency in regards to a customer satisfaction survey, since he works for a media service provider"). I recorded how she responded to the comments of online students (e.g., "Thanks for those [answers] out in cyberspace") and those of in-person students (e.g., "Frequency. Right. Now, moving on."). I noted how she solicited students' participation when they were silent (e.g., "Come on. Be brave! Shout it out!"). I recorded anything and everything I thought might matter, even observations that were only peripherally related at best—how she added sequences of numbers together, the icons she used in her presentation slides, and her advice for which calculators to use.

In retrospect, I read a sense of desperation in my initial field notes. I was flailing in the darkness, trying to put my hands on something that would be helpful. I grasped at what I could. Those first weeks in the field were disorienting. I was blinded by the absence of data that I imagined I was going to have and by observable phenomena whose meaning and relevance were unclear given a research question that was now in flux.

Resolving the First Blindness

Mercifully, my floundering was short-lived. By the 3rd week of observation, my eyes were beginning to adjust to their new environs, and I began to see differently. In part, this is because I began to relax. I loosened my grip on preconceived notions and trusted that I would be able to find something worth attending to—some story worth telling—even if it did not map neatly on my expectations. I began to look carefully at what was happening around me. I began to *explore*.

My exploration started by paying attention to the *what* of my environment. One concrete place to start was the environment itself. Each time I was in the field, I devoted a little time to describing the space I was in. We are curiously and unconsciously selective in what we attend to from all that is around us, and it was interesting to see how I noticed different aspects of the same space differently from week to week. One week some features stood out—the expansive whiteboard, the cream-and-blue-speckled linoleum floor, the errant vertical blind that refused to hang in parallel with the others. Another week, other details showed themselves—the wires hanging out of a mounted speaker, the condition of the all-in-one desk chairs, the cinder-block walls painted a bland off-white that begged to be ignored. Taken together, these fragments formed a composite picture for my readers of the spaces that provided the backdrop to my study. For example, I wrote of Dr. G.'s office:

> In contrast to the spaciousness and order of the classroom, Dr. G inhabits a cramped, disheveled office. The door is decorated with an eclectic collection of regalia from recent conferences, publications, and awards. Dr. G sits at a large metal desk that is covered with precarious piles of papers, folders, binders, and books—some rivaling the height of the computer monitor. Behind her is an overflowing bookshelf and second desk on which more piles compete for space with a printer, phone, and boxes. Except for a narrow corridor that accommodates a chair for a visitor, the floor is filled with stacks of books and boxes that contain file folders and loose papers.

I also wrote weekly descriptions of the *who* of the environment. I recorded who was present in the classroom and, partly in an effort to entertain myself during long evening classes, some novel description of the subjects. One week I described students' footwear; another week I focused on whether students wrote in notebooks, on loose-leaf papers, or on the presentation handouts. Another week, I recorded the beverages students sipped during the class. Hot or cold? Coffee or tea? Venti or grande? Throwaway or reusable? (Regardless of individual tastes, it does appear that studying statistics drives one to drink.) Of course, one's preference for a 20-ounce Starbucks coffee ultimately has little to do with his or her propensity to ask questions. However, these exercises helped me attend to some of the many, many details that remain hidden from our normal experience. When I focused on them, I found myself wondering about relevant information that before had escaped me. For example, in paying attention to footwear, I began to wonder about where the students had spent their day before coming to class: What were their professional lives like? What other responsibilities, in addition to weekly statistics homework and quizzes, filled their days and occupied their minds? How did individuals' lives outside of the classroom influence their participation in it? Was the high school principal in her sturdy, well-worn heels, who works 60-hour weeks and has little time to do the weekly reading, as apt to reveal that she was confused as the late-20-ish woman who appeared to have arrived straight from the gym, bounding into the classroom in a pair of Pumas? I was now in the realm of relevant information to question-asking. The process of looking closer and attending to detail helped me get there.

Similar to my weekly attention to the backdrop and actors that filled my observations, at the suggestion of Professor Horvat, I set specific goals for field observations. For example, one week I decided to pay attention to what immediately preceded students' questions in an attempt to illuminate what triggered questions. Another week, I focused on what students who were logged into the virtual classroom were experiencing, which revealed some frustrating technological hiccups that may have distracted from the learning process. On a smaller scale, I would take breaks from my normal field notes and hone in on a specific aspect of the environment, trying, for example, to describe the nonverbal aspect of students' speech or to describe students' movements as they listened to the lecture. These exercises proved useful in a variety ways. They allowed me to sample aspects of the environment for short periods of time. They broke up the tedium (yes, tedium) of field observations, distracting me with novel tasks. These novel tasks played an important role in expanding what I attended to in my environment, which on more than one occasion led to insight on the phenomenon of question-asking. In addition, when it came time to write the paper, the field notes that resulted from these goal-driven observation exercises formed a palette of detail-rich descriptions from which to paint a picture for my reader.

Close observation was key to exploration, but by itself was insufficient. Exploration involved considering different *meanings* and *implications* of the what and the who that I was observing. For me, this required assuming an exploratory mind-set. I needed to shift from trying to *find* meanings to *wondering* about them. I needed to welcome the notion that not knowing *what something means* was a very productive place to work from. It meant embracing ambiguity where I found it, and where I did not, seeking it out.

For me, this exploration involved a two-step process. The first step involved closely observing what happened around me, as I discussed above. The second critical step was to generate questions and speculate about the meaning of what I observed. As I mentioned earlier, this required that I suspend the automatic meanings I assigned to objects and actions and explore other possible meanings.

One strategy that helped me foster this reflective process was to include observer comments in my descriptive field notes. In many cases, I added these observer comments when I wrote up the field notes the following day. I viewed the task of writing up field notes as involving two elaborative tasks: (1) filling in details from the hurried fragments I had typed during the observation itself, and (2) speculating on what the observations meant relative to question-asking. The first step ensured I had good, extensive details to work with while the second step helped me to weave continual reflection and analysis into the process of observation. Professor Horvat reminded us often that more is more. For me this meant more descriptive observation *and* more ongoing reflection about what I was observing. Looking back on my observer comments, I see that most of the ideas that would appear in the final paper were generated in observer comments either during or immediately after time in the field. In contrast to quantitative analysis, the process of collecting data and making sense of it is interdependent and simultaneous.

Although they are intertwined, I was strongly encouraged to keep descriptive observations separate from my interpretation of the observations—to partition what was observable from what it might mean. Mimicking an example of field notes we had been shown, my running descriptive records—observations without interpretations—were justified to the left with a normal margin; when I made reflections on those observations, I indented the text, used italicized font, and began these reflections with the initials "O.C." for *Observer Comments*. This distinct formatting proved helpful in several ways. It allowed me to clearly distinguish between description and reflection, a process that was particularly helpful when it came to collecting my reflective thoughts for writing memos. The formatting differences also allowed me to easily monitor how much time and space I was allocating to describing what I was seeing compared to reflecting on it. On more than one occasion, seeing a wall of description reminded me that I also needed to explore possible meanings behind these descriptions. Observer comments ranged from approximately one-quarter to one-half of the total words in my field notes.

Observer comments aided my reflective process in several ways. Most commonly, they were a place to explore the possible meanings of the actions I was observing. The comments allowed me take a tiny sliver of action from the flurry of activity I observed and hold it up for close inspection. I fancied myself a 19th-century scientist, holding up a curious specimen to the light of a window. Examining a small bit of my objective descriptions was a mechanism for me to wonder what meanings were contained in the small granule of human behavior. In my experience, this was consistently fruitful. When I granted time, attention, and gravity to some small speck of the experience I had observed, I found within it a wondrous complexity.

For example, during a class meeting early in the semester, Dr. G explained to the students that optional homework assignments "signal the kinds of calculations you will be asked to do on tests and quizzes." When I considered this seemingly innocuous statement more closely in an observer comment, I wondered how messages about assessment and accountability influenced questions in the classroom:

> O.C. [Observer Comments]: These types of comments provide students with the nuts and bolts of how they will be assessed. It may convey another message as well: Pay attention to this because it will be on the test. This orientation toward testing can change how students approach and process the material. This likely depends on students' goals, but it is possible that it shapes their goals in subtle ways as well. What are students' goals for this course? What do they want to leave the course with?

Two characteristics of the observer comment above are worth highlighting. First, it demonstrates how I used these comments to explore possible meanings of actions. A message from the professor about how to study for the exam *might* result in shaping the goals of students and consequently their questioning behavior. To be sure, these types of comments are speculative. The Latin roots of the word *conjecture* combine the ideas of *together* and *throw*. For me, the observer comments were precisely about *throwing together* ideas and exploring possible connections. A second characteristic worth noting is how the act of throwing ideas together sometimes led to other unexpected and productive ideas. Many of my observer comments, like the ones above, were wandering, rambling freewrites. In their discursive style, they drift from one thought to the next, happening upon possible questions and connections. In the comment above, by pondering about how students interpret comments about assessment, I stumbled upon the idea of students' goals and how the classroom environment might shape these goals in subtle ways.

Many times, as with the example above, my musings suggested directions that ultimately the final project did not take. Other times, however, my chain of thought uncovered what would prove to be productive questions. For example, early in the semester, when a student arrived for office hours, I asked her if she minded if I sat in on her conversation with Dr. G. She responded, with a slight blush, "As long as you promise not to laugh." I assured her, "Nothing could be farther from the truth!" Later in the session, another student commented, "I have some easy questions and some more difficult ones. I'll start off with an easy one. Variance. I know how

to calculate it. I know what it is. But I don't know what I will use it for."
The following day, when I elaborated on my field notes, I reflected on these
exchanges:

> O.C. What makes her questions seem "easy" to her? What makes the others
> seem "more difficult"? How does she go about evaluating the easiness/
> hardness of her questions? . . . [and the] comment about laughing at
> questions, about the implicit laughability—or stupidity—of our questions
> is the central idea to this whole study. By drawing attention to her self-
> consciousness about her question, she may lower the cost of asking her
> questions. A question I should consider asking participants is if they ever
> worry about asking a "dumb question" and, if so, how they evaluate the
> "dumbness" of their question. . . . I should add a question about "stupid
> questions" to the interview.

In the comment above, I stumbled upon an idea that would be important in my final analysis of students' inhibitions to ask questions. In order to
assess the potential benefits and, especially, the costs of asking a question, I
argued, many students attempted but struggled to evaluate their questions
in terms of appropriateness, depth, helpfulness, and so on. Uncertain about
the value of their question for themselves and others, many students opted
to withhold or postpone asking. This embryonic idea, which resulted from
a close reflection of two students' casual remarks, led to questions and ideas
that grew over the course of the project.

THE SECOND BLINDNESS

By my 4th week in the field, my questions were spreading like dandelions.
With every round of observations, I found myself more attuned to nuance
and consequently with more questions filling the pages of my field notes. An
ever-widening network of questions is the natural consequence of paying
close attention to any aspect of the physical or social world. Our environments are enormously intricate, our behaviors the product of a sophisticated web of influences. Whereas my first blindness was the result of an
overly narrow vision and a lack of attention to meaningful detail, my second
blindness was the consequence of the opposite: becoming highly sensitive
to subtlety, more adept at perceiving complexity and, importantly, more
exploratory with regard to the meanings.

This avalanche of questions was evident in my first memo. We were
asked to write memos every other week during the period of data collection. At Professor Horvat's suggestion, I decided to use the first memo to

take an inventory of the various research interests and questions that I had accumulated in the first 3 weeks in the field. I begin by reflecting on possible research questions.

> What is my research question? Presently, I have several possible research questions: How do students experience the act of asking questions to the instructor in different communication channels? How are these costs different from other kinds of communication (e.g., answering a question)? How do students perceive peers' questions? How do students decide to use the communication channels they do? How are perceived costs similar or different across communication channels? What triggers question formation? Initially, my research question specifically addressed the social cost of asking questions.

My initial research question had multiplied to become half a dozen questions. And it didn't stop there. The memo was riddled with many more questions. What should constitute a questioning incident for this research? Did students even have many questions in their minds or did they experience unarticulated perplexity? Why did students ask fewer questions during class than they did in e-mails? How did group size and dynamics influence who asked questions and why? How did different learning activities influence questioning behavior uniquely? How could a researcher know the goal of the question for the asker? How did students evaluate their questions? In addition, I raised questions about differing levels of ability and confidence, the role of technological frustrations, students' goals for the course, how one student's question might affect another's questions, how different channels of communication interact with each other, the relationship of questioning to nonquestioning forms of participation, patterns of questions in relation to homework and quiz due dates, and students' perceptions of teacher availability.

In response to this deluge of questions, Professor Horvat responded at the end of my first memo, "Oh my—so much to respond to . . . I am not sure where to begin. There are many interesting things happening in this study. I guess at heart I think that there are too many." I had generated *too many* questions. She went on to explain:

> What I mean is that you really need to think through what you can address in the class and what remains for the future. There is enough here to fuel a whole career let alone just a dissertation. I think that you need to figure out what is the most important thing to BEGIN with—what do you need to understand before you can get to all of these questions? What question needs to be answered so that you can answer others? That is where I would start and how I would begin to think about honing my focus.

I was swimming in questions. To my mind, this was a good thing. Asking questions came easily to me and I enjoyed the process of wondering. In the back of my mind, I knew my questions would eventually have to be whittled down. I noted in the first memo that "not all of these questions can be answered in this study." Yet I was naive in imagining what I could accomplish in a semester. In what I thought was a gesture of self-awareness and constraint, I commented that "I will need to focus on a subset of them." In retrospect, my acknowledgment of the need to partially restrict my questions is laughable. A subset!? It would become clear that given the restrictions of the course and the assignment, a subset was far too great a bite to chew. "Choose one," Professor Horvat advised. "It's hard enough to answer one question in twenty pages."

THE THIRD BLINDNESS

It was very challenging for me to choose just one question. By nature, I am drawn toward possibilities, potential, and what can be. Choosing one research question meant saying "no" to many possibilities. It meant saying "later" to interests that seemed pressing. This was a difficult process because I had invested time and intellectual energy into these budding ideas. I was carefully cultivating them. I was rooting for them. Now I had to cut them off at the stem so that one could mature. Whereas my first blindness was resolved through exploration, my second blindness was resolved through focus. Focus required that I blinded myself to some possibilities for the sake of others. Sharp focus sacrificed breadth for depth, the many for the one, the peripheral for the singular.

But which question? Professor Horvat had given me some advice on the process of choosing, by asking me, "Which seems to be the most compelling and answerable at this point?" Her question stuck with me because it contained several important notions necessary to the process of selecting focus. First, "which" suggested choosing from an array of options, not a call for more possibilities to be put on the table. Second, "at this point" conveyed the notion that this process was ongoing and continually informed by new data that was being collected. Third, she suggested I select the question that was "the most compelling and answerable." These elements are woven through my description of how I ultimately arrived at my research question.

"First questions first," Professor Horvat suggested, encouraging me to consider the one question that could precede the others in a larger line of research, which I might address over several years. Yet I saw no obvious starting point. Do I start with what triggers questions? Or what inhibits questions that are already triggered for people? Do I understand questions in classrooms better by comparing them with questions asked in other situations, or should they first be understood by themselves and then later compared?

I considered my goals for the project and prospective audiences. I was hoping to submit what I produced for a professional conference. So as I evaluated possible research questions, I considered an audience wider than Professor Horvat, and a purpose beyond the course requirements. Yet this did little to limit the field of options, since many of the questions seemed compelling and potentially relevant for a larger audience.

In my long list of questions, I identified two sets of questions. One set of questions related to perceptions of asking questions in the classroom during class meetings. This set included students' perception of their own questions, the questions of their peers, and why they withheld questions during class. A second set of questions involved comparing question-asking in different contexts. These questions explored the differences between online and in-person students, between electronic and in-person communication, and in asking contexts like classroom and office hours. This set of questions grew out of the uniqueness of the hybrid/parallel online and in-person class structure. After all, this was why I had chosen this research site, because it allowed me a unique comparison across in-person and online students and face-to-face and virtual forms of communication.

Yet when I reflected on it, I had little data that related to the latter set of questions. Who were these online students? They were largely unknown to me. My field notes were based on observations in class meetings and office hours. Since few online students logged into the virtual classroom during those meetings and because I did not yet have access to e-mails, the online students and e-mailed questions existed only as potential sources of data. They had not yet materialized.

By contrast, when I considered the set of questions about students' perceptions of questions during class meetings, I found I had more data with which to work. Although students had asked few questions, I was beginning to collect a large amount of descriptive data on the classroom context. I was beginning to be able to describe what the classroom and office hours looked and sounded like, and to describe the patterns of behavior that I was beginning to notice in these contexts.

Yet this set of research questions revolved around students' *perceptions* of asking questions in this context. I had virtually no data on this at all. In my first memo, I noted:

> I am concerned that I am not collecting the kinds of data I need regarding students' experience. In order to answer these questions, I need to devote more time to talking with individuals about their experience. Observation alone cannot answer my question about students' perceptions.

In the subsequent memo, Professor Horvat responded to this concern, emphasizing that my observations of the classroom environment "frames question-asking." She continued:

> Observations alone do not answer your question but it has been interesting to see how the atmosphere of the class may affect the behavior. I think this is important because if we are looking to tell instructors about how they can increase question-asking on the part of students, one of the only things they can control is what happens in the room and they are in control of a good bit of it.

I resolved to start interviewing students about their experiences. I was surprised at how hesitant I was to interview students. For a person interested in studying individuals' inhibitions to asking questions, I was curiously and self-consciously aware of my own inhibition to ask students about their experience. This inhibition stemmed in part from my reluctance to impede upon their time. These were students attending an evening course in statistics, most of whom arrived after a full day of work. I felt uncomfortable asking students to arrive half an hour earlier or stay after class to talk with me.

More than the imposition, however, I felt self-conscious about asking students to tell me about their experience of asking questions. Sitting face-to-face with a peer and asking them to describe what they were thinking and feeling when they asked questions felt silly. I was publicly attributing weight to an act that we often dismiss as mundane and normal. Maybe there was nothing interesting to the act of asking at all. Maybe all my conjecture and speculation was only that. Here I was probing about students' thoughts and feelings. In retrospect, I see that in interviewing students about their perceptions of their questions, I was afraid of asking my own dumb questions!

I knew I had to dive in. After the fourth class meeting, an opportunity presented itself that helped me take the first step. T., one of two students who posed questions during the preceding class meeting, remained in the class occupying himself on his phone as others, including Dr. G., left the room. Alone, I sheepishly asked if he had a couple of minutes to talk with me about the project. "Sure," he replied. With his consent, I recorded our conversation on my phone. Using an interview protocol I had drafted, I began asking him about the question he'd asked in class. I repeated his question verbatim, reminding him of what had just transpired in the class before he asked it. "Can you tell me everything you were thinking and feeling from the moment that question entered your mind through the point when you heard the answer?" I asked. He paused. His response would shape the research question and the direction of the study.

"Yes, I remember it clearly." He described what prompted the question for him and how he initially tried to look for the answer on the previous presentation slides. He described weighing potential benefits of asking his question while entertaining the possibility that he may be interrupting, and how he considered his personal interest in the question in light of how relevant he perceived the question to be for his peers. He explained how his perceptions of the instructors' goals influenced whether he thought his question was an "appropriate interruption." When I asked him about a specific question a peer had asked, he explained how it had reframed his thinking on the topic, raising issues and questions of which he was previously unaware. The interview went on to reveal that although he decided to ask a question during class, there were many others that he decided not to ask. He described wondering if he could first try to figure out the answer for himself before asking it in class and explained his reticence to ask certain questions, believing that the professor would try to answer it too quickly so as not to waste time. He expressed his concern not to unduly slow the group learning process.

I felt like I had won the lottery. A single 20-minute interview revealed an enormous richness of psychological processing that occurred as one student considered asking his questions. If my first interview was any guide, there was much to be explored—both for why students asked and why students withheld their questions during class meetings. The small number of students' questions that were posed during class meetings and office hours were the tip of the iceberg. Lurking underneath was a complex world of decisions that I had intuited—and hoped—was there. Now I had some evidence that suggested these would be waters worth wading.

In light of the initial interview data, I reevaluated my research questions. I was leaning against pursuing a question about *how* students asked their questions (e.g., e-mail vs. office hours). Instead, I was leaning toward one of two questions: (1) Why did students choose to ask or withhold their questions? and (2) How did students perceive the questions of their peers and what impact did this have on their learning? In my field notes after the 4th week, I weighed my interest in and supporting evidence for two remaining questions. Of the first question, I wrote:

> There is evidence—especially from T.'s and M.'s interview—that begins to address parts of a question [about the inhibition to ask questions], specifically, how do students experience the act of asking questions to the instructor in class and during office hours? What's missing is data about students' experience e-mailing the instructor and chatting questions online. I need to decide if I will seek interviews with virtual students so as to include these communication channels in the research question, or alter the research question to exclude e-mails and chats.

The question regarding perception of peers' questions, I wrote,

> continues to be a contender. The only information I have on this comes
> from T.'s interview, and it would require that I conduct a lot more interviews.
> However, I think I would like interviews to play a larger role in the project
> moving forward. I would like to continue to observe what questions are
> being asked and what is triggering them (during class meetings and office
> hours), but I would like for more of my time to be spent exploring students'
> perceptions through interviews.

The field of possible questions was narrowing. What had become clear was
the need to gather more interview data and see where it led.

I resolved to interview two students each week, one from the in-person
section and another from the online section. I began with students who had
asked questions during the class meeting. At the time, I did not know if
those students who did not ask questions simply did not have any questions,
or else chose to withhold them. As I accumulated evidence that question
askers regularly withheld some of their questions, I expanded my pool of interviewees. By the end of the course, I had interviewed a total of 18 students,
which included all students enrolled in the in-person class and all five of the
online students who had accepted my request for an interview.

I revised my protocol to focus on the two research questions I described
above. For students who attended class meetings either in person or virtually, I began by asking about their decision to ask a question (if they had),
followed by an exploration of the questions they had but did not ask. I then
asked students about their perceptions of specific questions asked by their
peers. Last on the protocol was a set of more general questions, including
how comfortable they felt asking questions in general to Dr. G and how
question-asking was different in e-mails and office hours.

For all but the last section of the protocol, I attempted to stimulate
students' ability to recall by repeating back their question verbatim and describing the context in which they had asked their question. In most cases,
especially for interviews that were conducted immediately after the class,
students were able to provide rich and vivid detail about their thoughts and
feelings as they evaluated their questions and made decisions about asking
or withholding their questions, and about their perceptions of their peers'
questions. By contrast, the last section of the interview, addressing students'
general experience, often produced vague, detail-impoverished descriptions
of how they generally experienced the atmosphere of the class.

Since this was the only part of the protocol that pertained to online
students who did not log in in real time and because these students were
less responsive to my invitations to conduct interviews, I began to focus on
question-asking during class meetings.

By the 5th week in the field, I had abandoned my research question relating to comparing student types and asking contexts. With too little data and such promising alternatives, it had become clear this was neither the most viable nor the most compelling question. I would focus, instead, on the questions of students in the in-person section.

For our second memo, we were tasked with selecting a research question (even if it would not be *the* research question), identifying a few concepts that address the question, and supporting these ideas with evidence. I selected the following question: What inhibits students from asking questions to the instructor while learning introductory statistics? I noted that the initial interview data suggested many possible themes, including:

1. a preference to answer their questions on their own;
2. how available the instructor was perceived to be;
3. concerns for peers' learning;
4. consideration of the instructor's goals;
5. not having a clearly formulated question; and
6. how prepared the student felt.

Professor Horvat noted that they "seem to resonate with the data." The initial interviews suggested many themes that seemed promising. Yet they rested fragilely on a thin wafer of evidence, a handful of interview responses from five students. Professor Horvat had explained that answers to research questions were most convincingly answered when researchers could draw evidence from various sources to argue their point. For example, triangulating multiple interviewees' responses with observational data makes a stronger case than a single, isolated quotation. I did not have this yet, and worried that my evidence for these claims would remain weak.

In addition, even as my second memo concluded that focusing on students' inhibitions to asking question in class was a promising way forward, I continued to be nagged by a competing interest in how students perceived their peers' questions. For example, I was cumulating evidence that contradicted the old teaching adage, "you should ask *your* question because others have the *same* question." In fact, the students whom I interviewed rarely had their peers' question already in their mind when it was asked. Something more interesting was occurring. In an observer comment, I wrote,

> What might really be happening is that the question is not simultaneously in the heads of peers until the question is asked. Then students realize that they also do not know the answer, and *now* have the question in their mind.

It appeared that peers' questions triggered awareness that what they previously understood was incomplete. Peers' questions appeared to help students become cognizant of what they did not know. It was question contagion. "So, the new proverb might go," I continued, "'If you have a question, you should ask it, so that others will have that question, too.' This is just a hunch, and I need to continue to ask this question to interviewees." This idea intrigued me and, viable as my other research question seemed to be, I kept pursuing this one as well.

As we were asked to consider wrapping up our time in the field, I continued to grapple with the choice between two questions: "What meaning do students make of their peers' questions?" and "How do students decide to ask or withhold their questions to the instructor?" In my field notes of the 5th and 6th week, I considered the possibility of combining the two questions, with the possible phrasing, "How do students perceive the role of student-generated questions in classroom discourse?" To my ear, the wording suggested a focus on perceptions of others' questions, even though it was clear the perceptions of students' own questions would constitute a large part of the paper. The more important problem, however, was that although the phrasing semantically combined the two original questions into a single question, in reality they were separate questions. A single paper would do justice to neither.

Despite a great deal of fretting and fussing, second-guessing and bet-hedging—and, I suspect, because of it—the decision in the end was surprisingly easy. When, after 6 weeks, I surveyed my data, it overwhelmingly pointed to how students decide to ask or withhold their questions in class. This was the story I could most easily, most fully, and most compellingly tell. I had my question. My blinders were on.

Well, almost. I continued collecting data through the end of the semester. For the remaining weeks in the field, I collected data on perceptions of peers' questions as well as my central research question. However, this now felt like reconnaissance for a future study rather than data for the present project. Although I continued to conduct interviews, even as I prepared the final paper and poster for the class, by the 6th week I had collected the majority of the data with which I would write the report for the class. Research question and data in hand, it was time to put the pieces together.

Resolving the Third Blindness: Figure and Ground

The process of closing in on my research question—of blinding myself to alternative directions—was gradual and hard-won. Curiously, no sooner than I'd gotten the blinders on was I tasked with a new challenge: situating the singular focus within a larger context. This required another shift in thinking and a new way of seeing the phenomenon. I found the terminology from the visual arts to be helpful. Visual artists use the terms *figure* and *ground* to describe the design element that contrasts objects (i.e., figure) with the space around them (i.e., ground), encouraging our eyes to make a distinction between them. Those elements in two-dimensional space that attract our most acute attention and that we interpret as three-dimensional are referred to as the *figure*. These are data that, honed through a research question, play the most prominent role in the picture we are creating. *Ground,* on the other hand, refers to the space around the figure, which through contrast defines the boundaries of the figure. These are the data that provide the context—the back*ground*—to the story we tell.

After working so hard to restrict my vision to focus on inhibitions, I found the process of describing my phenomenon in the larger context to be happily integrative and holistic. Now I had the chance to tie together many earlier interests and observations that had been sidelined. False starts and abandoned directions became useful tools for making the *figure* stand out from the *ground*.

Two examples from the final project will help to illustrate this point. One of the reasons why students withheld their questions from the instructor was that they were concerned that in asking their question, they would unnecessarily impinge on the learning of their peers. Asking a question meant that the instructor would need to take time away from "covering the material" to address their question, and this had the potential to interfere, slow, or otherwise impede peers' learning process. Yet in my exploration of students' perceptions of peers' questions—a research question that ultimately was abandoned—I had learned that students consistently described peers' questions as "helpful." Because peers' questions often helped students see gaps in their own knowledge, peers' questions, far from impeding their learning, actually assisted it. Using this data, I contrasted students' inhibitory perceptions of their own questions with their appreciation for peers' questions. In the final paper, I discussed the implications of this contrast. If greater emphasis were to be placed on the positive role peers' questions play in aiding others' learning, perhaps this would lower students' inhibitions to asking their own questions.

In another example, an early research question—What triggers students' questions?—shaped the story I told about students' inhibitions. In collecting data for this question, I had noticed, for example, that students generated far more questions during small-group activities than during weekly lectures. I used these data to discuss why students' inhibitions changed in response to contextual cues in the classroom. I argued that inhibitions decreased when the benefits of asking were perceived to outweigh the costs. For example, in small-group activities the utility of asking a question increased because it served an immediate purpose in the problem-solving task; at the same time, the costs attributed to asking a question, such as interrupting, appeared to be minimized. As benefits outweighed costs, students were less likely to inhibit their questions. In the final paper, I considered the implications of teachers' actions and activity characteristics in terms of encouraging and discouraging questioning behavior.

I share these examples to suggest that all of the exploration and tinkering, all of the soul-searching and decisions, all of the forgone and lost opportunities—well, in the end, they are not so lost. Ultimately, the picture we paint requires rich details against which we can contrast the story we have chosen to highlight.

HOPES AND FEARS OF SEEING

What I hope has become clear from the description of my process of generating and selecting research questions is that the task requires building a wide range of skills. Like sets of muscles, each is uniquely useful in completing certain tasks. At times, we need to extend and expand what we see in the field. Other times, we need to constrain and contract our focus. These skills are complementary, even as they are in tension with each other. Before embarking on the journey of qualitative research, it can be helpful to understand the necessary skills before we apply them, though in the end, like all skills, they are developed nearly exclusively through practice. There is no substitute for experience.

Sitting in a large circle during the first meeting of the qualitative course, each student was asked to share a hope and a fear for the course. I started with my fear. I explained that I feared that I would find what Gertrude Stein found when she returned to her childhood home: "There is no there, there." I had invested a sizeable portion of my coursework in exploring issues related to student-generated questions. I had explored the theoretical and empirical literature. I had a reasonable idea of the areas in which the field could benefit from further study. But against the backdrop of all that preparation, I had a strong fear that it would all turn out to be a dead end—a boring story with an obvious conclusion. In reflecting back, I think I had an elementary lesson to learn about the nature of qualitative research. It is, fundamentally, exploratory. And persistent exploration nearly always leads to discovery. It does not, however, necessarily lead to confirmation. I think this is what I was getting at when I expressed this fear: What if things are not as I think they are? What if there is not a "'there" where I think it ought to be? That, well, seems like a fear that is likely to be realized many times over, and one that, at its heart, bucks the true nature of what it means to question.

I followed my fear with a hope. I hoped that my work during the semester would lead to a product that I would be able to build on after the course was complete. As I fumbled, explored, and struggled through the process, the goal of producing something that would be useful to others was very important for me. What I said of my fear also applies to my hope. With persistence and patience, the process of looking closely will lead to a story worth telling. For in the end, when we approach a phenomenon that is important to us, that we believe has value to others, and we do so thoughtfully, methodically, open-mindedly, reflectively, and with the help of knowledgeable others, the deck is stacked in our favor from our very first question.

NOTES

1. An Institutional Review Board (IRB) is an official office of a university that oversees that research conducted under the auspices of the institution meet ethical and legal standards for research. In addition to university-wide review processes, the department responsible for the course on Institutional Racism had an additional review process.

2. Expectancy-Value Theory is a motivational theory that posits that an individual's choice to engage in a task is shaped by (1) the extent to which one expects to be successful in the task and (2) the extent to which the task is valued.

Appendix

Site Selection Guidelines and Site Prospectus Guidelines

The core activity of this course is an independent data collection and analysis project that will be carried out by each student. Each student will be required to find a site where he or she will collect data over about a 7-week period. Below you will find the Site Selection Guidelines, which outline the specifications for your site as well as the requirements for the Site Selection Prospectus, a document that you will turn in on or before the second class meeting.

Many students have a tough time finding a site with many false starts and dead ends. The site must be new to you, and should be a place where you will be able to spend 3 to 4 hours each week observing. It is a very good idea to have identified a potential site or two *prior to* the first class meeting. I would be pleased to discuss potential sites with students prior to the start of the class. I must approve your site prospectus prior to the start of fieldwork. I would be happy to review this document prior to the start of class in order to facilitate a smooth entry into fieldwork.

SITE SELECTION GUIDELINES: SOME THINGS TO CONSIDER

Choose a Well-Defined Site

In general, your site should be a physical space that is relatively well-defined. You do not want to choose a site that is too open or unbounded. It should also be a place that is relatively new or novel for you as an observer. Part of the experience of doing fieldwork has to do with negotiating access at the site and learning about a place for the first time as you observe.

Select a Site That Has Some Regular Activity

You also want to select a place that has some continuity to its activities. Though each day at the site need not be exactly the same as another, there does need to be some continuity of activity. In addition, you will be wise to select a site that has ongoing interaction among people—there needs to be enough activity to observe.

Select a Site Where You Can Gain Access

You should also select a site where you can gain access. You do not necessarily need to know someone "on the inside" in order to gain access. However, beware of selecting a site to which it will be difficult to gain access or one that will not allow you the kind of access you require.

Select a Site That Is Interesting to You

You also want to select a place where you will like to spend a good deal of time. So the site needs to be interesting and a place where you can envision yourself hanging out for a significant amount of time.

SITE PROSPECTUS GUIDELINES DUE PRIOR TO THE START OF FIELDWORK

The Site Selection Prospectus should be between one and two pages. Based on this prospectus, I will approve your site for the course. You should give me an idea of who, what, where, and why, regarding your site. Specifically, I want to know:

Who Will You Observe?

Tell me what you can about the people you will be observing. Are they students, educators, health care workers, administrators, and so on? Why are they at this site? What is their function? Are they old or young? Male or female? Try to give me as much detail about them as possible. There may be many individuals at a given site and you may not be observing all of them but only some of them. Identify who you will observe.

What Will You Observe?

Though the answer to this question will probably change over time as you develop and refine your research question, I want you to give me some idea of what activity you will observe. What activity is occurring at this site?

Where Will You Observe?

What will be the physical site of your observations? Will it be in one well-defined place such as an office or restaurant? How will you define, at least initially, the physical boundaries of the site?

Why Will You Be Observing at This Site?

Usually social scientists observe at a particular site because they want to answer a research question or questions. You might not have a specific research question yet but I would like to know why you are choosing this particular site. Why do you want to spend many hours observing at this site and what do you hope to gain by doing so?

References

Cazet, D. (1990). *Never spit on your shoes*. New York: Scholastic.

Csikszentmihalyi, M. (1997). *Finding flow: The psychology of engagement with every day life*. New York: Basic Books.

Cucchiara, M., & Horvat, E. M. (2009). Perils and promises: Middle-class parental involvement in urban schools. *American Educational Research Journal, 46*(4), 974–1004.

Fine, M. (1991). *Framing dropouts: Notes on the politics on an urban public high school*. Albany: State University of New York Press.

Frank, C. (1999). *Ethnographic eyes: A teacher's guide to classroom observation*. Portsmouth, NH: Heineman.

Goffman, E. (1967). *Interaction ritual: Essays in face-to-face behavior*. Chicago: Aldine Publishing Co.

Guba, E. G., & Lincoln, Y. S. (1994). Competing paradigms in qualitative research. In N. K. Denzin & Y. S. Lincoln (Eds.), *Handbook of qualitative research* (pp. 105–117). London: Sage.

Hesse-Biber, S. N., & Leavy, P. (2006). *The practice of qualitative research*. Thousand Oaks, CA: Sage.

Horvat, E. M., & Davis, J. E. (2011). Schools as sites for transformation: Exploring the contribution of the habitus. *Youth and Society, 43*(1), 142–170.

Kubler-Ross, E. (1997). *On death and dying*. New York: Scribner Classics.

Lareau, A. (2011). *Unequal childhoods* (2nd ed.). Berkeley: University of California Press.

Lareau, A., & Shultz, J. (Eds.). (1996). *Journeys through ethnography: Realistic accounts of fieldwork*. Boulder, CO: Westview Press.

Lerher, J. (2012). *Imagine: How creativity works*. New York: Houghton, Mifflin Harcourt.

Oldenburg, R. (1999). *The great good place: Cafes, coffee shops, bookstores, bars, hair salons and other hangouts at the heart of a community*. Cambridge, MA: DaCapo Press.

Seidman, I. (2013). *Interviewing as qualitative research: A guide for researchers in education and social sciences* (4th ed.). New York: Teachers College Press.

Simon, B. (2009). *Everything but the coffee: Learning about America from Starbucks*. Los Angeles: University of California Press.

Willis, J. W. (2007). *Foundations of qualitative research: Interpretive and critical approaches*. Thousand Oaks, CA: Sage.

Whyte, W. F. (1993). *Street corner society: The social structure of an Italian slum*. Chicago: University of Chicago Press. (Original work published 1943)

Index

About the Authors

Erin Horvat is associate professor of urban education in the department of teaching and learning at the College of Education, Temple University, in Philadelphia. As a sociologist of education, she aims to use research to illustrate how educational institutions create and reproduce inequality throughout the educational pipeline. As an educational activist and practitioner, she has worked for many years with YouthBuild Philadelphia Charter School to provide access to educational opportunity for out-of-school youth. With Carla O'Connor she is the editor of *Beyond Acting White: ReFraming the Debate on Black Student Achievement.*

Emily Tancredi-Brice Agbenyega is a doctoral student in urban education at Temple University. Her current research interests center on the process of youth becoming protagonists of their education, particularly in underserved communities, and how youth negotiate this process in relation to dominant discourses on youth in society.

Bradley W. Bergey is a doctoral student in educational psychology at Temple University. Drawing on a decade of teaching experience in secondary schools in the United States, Mexico, and Spain, his research focuses on student engagement in classroom settings and aims to support student-directed and interest-driven learning.

Mary Lou Heron is a graduate student in the College of Education at Temple University, enrolled in the Ph.D. Literacy and Learners Program. Her research interests include examining oral language development and its contribution to reading comprehension. She works as a literacy consultant at the Northeastern Educational Intermediate Unit in Pennsylvania.